The
Splendor
of the
Temple

A Pictorial Guide To Herod's Temple
and its Ceremonies

ALEC GARRARD

Text © 2000 Alec Garrard
This edition copyright
© 2000 Angus Hudson Ltd/
Tim Dowley & Peter Wyart
trading as Three's Company
All plans and diagrams ©
copyright 2000 Alec Garrard

First published in the USA 2000
by Kregel Pblications, a division
of Kregel, Inc., P.O. Box 2607,
Grand Rapids, MI 49501. Kregel
Publications provides trusted,
biblical publications for
Christian growth and service.
Your comments and suggestions
are valued.

The Splendor of the Temple was
previously published in a
different edition by Moat Farm
Publications in 1997.

Edited by Tim Dowley
Designed by Peter Wyart,
Three's Company

Worldwide coedition organized
and produced by Angus
Hudson Ltd, Concorde House,
Grenville Place, Mill Hill,
London NW7 3SA, England
Tel: +44 20 8959 3668
Fax: +44 20 8959 3678

ISBN 0-8254-2697-9

Printed in Singapore

Picture acknowledgments
All photographs by the author
except as follows:
Tim Dowley: pp. 7, 16, 20 inset,
91
Angus Hudson Ltd/Three's
Company: pp. 24/5, 36/7, 76/7
Zev Radovan: pp. 28, 42, 82
Peter Wyart: pp. 13, 87, 90

Contents

Also Available from Kregel Publications

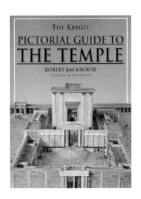

The Kregel Pictorial Guide to the Temple
Robert Backhouse • 0-8254-3039-9, 32 pp., paperback, full color

The grandeur and day-to-day activities of Herod's magnificent temple have been brought back t life. Complete with full-color illustrations and photographs of a detailed scale model of the temple

> "This volume is a worthwhile addition to your library, and its use will greatly enhance your understanding of the structures that the Scriptures devote much space to detailing."
> —*Messenger*

The Temple: Its Ministry and Service As They Were at the Time of Jesus Christ
Alfred Edersheim • 0-8254-2509-3, 256 pp., hardcover, full color

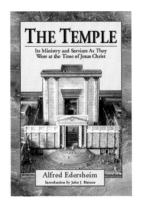

This classic work on the ministry of the first-century temple has now been reset and expanded wit full-color photographs, maps, and charts! This edition features the exclusive photographs of a mag nificently detailed scale model of the temple and temple grounds created by Mr. Alec Garrard c Norfolk, England.

> "One of the most beautifully crafted editions of this work ever to appear. . . . lavishly illustrated."
> —J. Randall Price, President
> World of the Bible Ministries

Eusebius: The Church History
Paul L. Maier, translator • 0-8254-3328-2, 416 pp., hardcover, full color

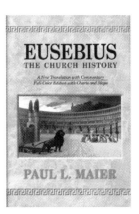

Beginning with Jesus of Nazareth and ending with Constantine the Great, the first Christian en peror, Eusebius presents a panorama of apostles, church fathers, elders, bishops, heroes, heretic confessors, and martyrs. Key features in the edition include: more than 1,250 color photograph maps, and illustrations; an informative introduction to Eusebius and his works; and commentarie of significant historical developments.

> "There is no book more important to understanding the early church than Eusebius's *Church History*. And there is no edition more readable and engaging than this one."
> —Mark Galli, Editor
> *Christian History*

Josephus: The Essential Works
Paul L. Maier, translator • 0-8254-3260-x, 416 pp., hardcover, full color

Josephus offers the greatest source of information on first-century biblical history outside of th New Testament. The most important writings of Josephus have been carefully and newly translate by Dr. Paul L. Maier.

This award-winning work contains condensed sections of *Jewish Antiquities* and *The Jewis War,* and is accompanied by insightful commentary and full-color photographs that bring to life th people and places of Jewish and Christian history. With 91 full-color photographs, 21 maps an charts, and 19 sidebar discussions, this is the essential version of the essential *Josephus.*

> "I am delighted to welcome this abridged edition which preserves the essential *Josephus.* I commend it warmly."
> —F. F. Bruce

Introduction

The Second Temple, built on Jerusalem's Temple Mount by Herod the Great between 19 B.C. and A.D. 4, was, in fact, a grand extension and refurbishment of an earlier temple on this site and was undoubtedly one of the most remarkable and beautiful buildings of ancient times. But as it was almost totally destroyed by the Roman army when they put down the Jewish revolt in A.D. 70, leaving only minimal evidence behind, it has barely featured in our mental picture of ancient times, in the way that the pyramids and temples of ancient Egypt and the buildings of classical Greece and Rome have done.

During three years of careful research and fourteen years of painstaking construction, I have created as accurate a replica of the Second Temple as is possible from the available written and archaeological evidence. This has enabled me to produce in turn the realistic exterior and interior photographs that illustrate this book. Since the original buildings no longer exist, this is, of course, the only way of creating such views.

I have been a model maker from my youth, when I constructed replicas of planes and ships. As my interest turned to biblical subjects, I became fascinated first by the tabernacle and made a model

The author, Alec Garrard, is a Suffolk farmer, who has devoted some eighteen years to creating this unique scale model of Herod's Temple.

A Brief Chronology of Jerusalem

?	Tabernacle
?	Solomon's Temple built
?	Plundered by Egyptians
587 B.C.	Destroyed by Babylonians
537 B.C.	Restored by Ezra and Nehemiah: Building of Second Temple
537–515 B.C.	Rebuilt under Zerubbabel
167 B.C.	Desecrated by Antiochus IV
164 B.C.	Altar rededicated Hasmonean extension of Temple
63 B.C.	Romans capture Jerusalem
37 B.C.	Herod becomes King of Israel
19 B.C.	Herod starts to rebuild Temple
A.D. 70	Romans sack Jerusalem and destroy the Temple
A.D. 638	Muslims capture Temple site
A.D. 691/2	Muslims build Dome of the Rock
1099	Crusaders capture Jerusalem
1187	Mamluks capture Jerusalem
1517	Ottoman Turks rule Jerusalem
1917	British Mandate of Palestine
1948	State of Israel founded
1967	Six Day War

of it in 1977 measuring 70 x 135 centimeters (twenty-seven by fifty-five inches). Stimulated by the success of this model, I conceived the more ambitious project of building a large scale model of Herod's Temple.

I began research for the temple model in 1980, commenced construction in 1983—yet even now I am making alterations as new evidence appears! It measures 6 x 3.6 meters (twenty feet by twelve feet) in area and is built of baked clay "stones" upon a wooden framework, to make it as authentic as possible. To bring the building to life and to illustrate the activities that went on in it, I have made some four thousand model human figures, again of baked clay, hand-painted in their correct costumes and placed where they would have been engaged in the life of the temple in the first century.

I hope this book will be of interest to scholars and casual readers alike and be valued as a reliable record of the appearance of the Second Temple, subject to any changes made necessary by future archaeological discoveries.

Alec Garrard, 1999

The Dome of the Rock today occupies the site of Herod's Temple in Jerusalem.

1. A Brief History of the Temple

The story of the Jewish temple begins almost thirty-five hundred years ago, when Moses led the children of Israel out of Egypt to freedom. As they journeyed through the wilderness on their way to the Promised Land, the Hebrews discovered that their new-found liberty was not the unmixed blessing that they had expected; it brought with it responsibilities, both to God and to their fellow human beings. The Hebrew people encountered many obstacles and many new problems, all of which they had to resolve.

It was in these circumstances that God gave Moses the Ten Commandments and set out the covenant that he promised to keep with his people (Exodus 19–24). Alongside many regulations about worship and guidance about how his people should behave toward each other, God also gave detailed instructions for building a great tent, which we know as the tabernacle— a sacred place to which the Israelites would come to worship and present their sacrifices. Moses was given full instructions about the dimensions of the tabernacle, the materials from which it was to be constructed, and precisely how the various sacrifices were to be offered (Exodus 25–31).

The tabernacle was, in effect, a portable temple, which the people could set up wherever they halted and which could be used for worship as long as they remained in that place. The tabernacle was a large tent measuring 13.7 x 4.6 meters (45 x 15 feet). It had two rooms, a larger, outer room called the Holy Place, into which only priests were permitted; and an inner room, called the Holy of Holies, or the Holiest Place, where only the high priest entered only once a year, at Yom Kippur, the Day of Atonement. In the Holiest Place stood the ark of the covenant.

The idea of a portable temple was especially suitable as the Israelites traveled through the wilderness. When God directed his people to move on, the tabernacle was dismantled, carried with them, and reassembled at their next stopping place. This portable tabernacle served the children of Israel well as they traveled on through the wilderness toward the Promised Land.

When the Israelites finally arrived in the Promised Land, they set up the tabernacle on a permanent site at Shiloh, near present-day Nablus. This must have caused them new problems. As long as the tabernacle was moved from place to place, it was regularly erected on fresh, unpolluted soil; the blood and other waste products resulting from the many sacrifices made within it would be left behind when the Israelites moved on. But once the tabernacle was erected on a permanent site, the Israelites must have had to devise new methods for keeping its site clean.

The tabernacle served the Israelites as a place of worship for some three hundred and fifty years. It was moved from time to time, as they experienced first prosperity then defeat by their many enemies. The tabernacle and its contents were captured a number of times by their enemies and an equal number of times

Ground Plan of Herod's Temple

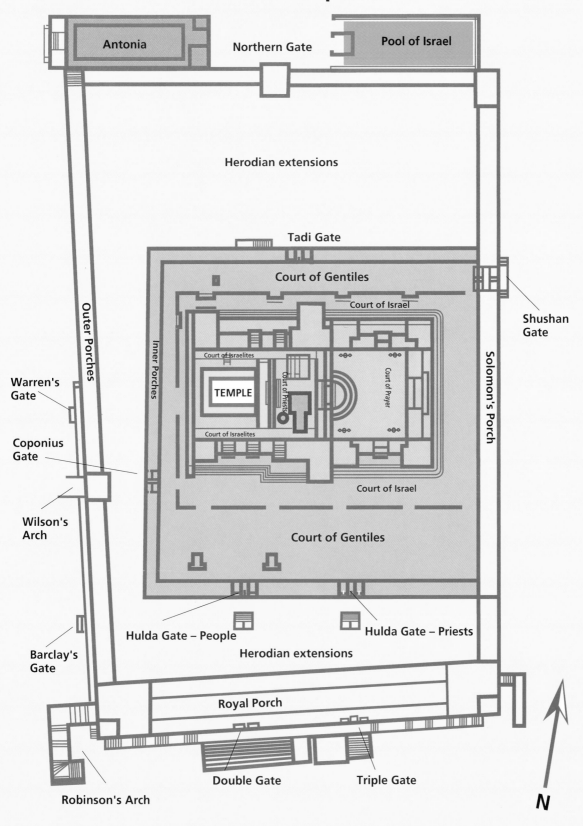

Antonia

Northern Gate

Pool of Israel

Herodian extensions

Tadi Gate

Court of Gentiles

Court of Israel

Outer Porches

Shushan Gate

Inner Porches

Court of Israelites

TEMPLE

Court of Priests

Court of Prayer

Warren's Gate

Coponius Gate

Wilson's Arch

Court of Israelites

Court of Israel

Solomon's Porch

Court of Gentiles

Barclay's Gate

Hulda Gate – People

Hulda Gate – Priests

Herodian extensions

Royal Porch

Robinson's Arch

Double Gate

Triple Gate

N

Note: Court of Prayer = Court of Women
Court of Israelites = Court of Men

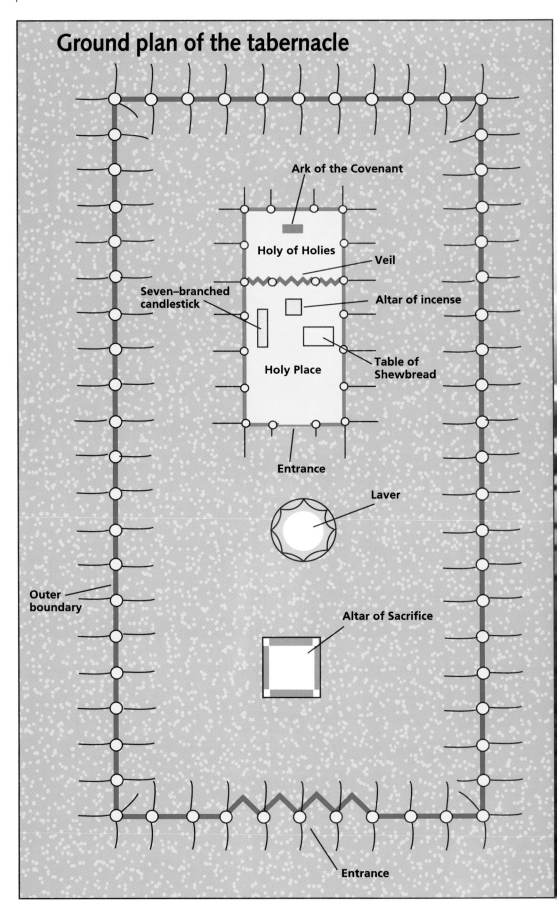

Ground plan of the tabernacle

Ark of the Covenant

Holy of Holies

Veil

Seven–branched candlestick

Altar of incense

Table of Shewbread

Holy Place

Entrance

Laver

Outer boundary

Altar of Sacrifice

Entrance

Alec Garrard's model of the tabernacle—a large tent measuring 13.7 x 4.6 meters (45 x 15 feet).

recovered. But the tabernacle continued to be used by the Israelites throughout this period of warfare and intertribal strife.

Finally, in about 1000 B.C., King David, after uniting the twelve tribes of Israel and defeating their hostile neighbors, proposed building a permanent temple. Meanwhile, the tabernacle was brought to the new Israelite capital, Jerusalem (1 Kings 8:1–5). David argued that it was wrong that, while the people now lived in houses of stone, God's house remained a mere tent (2 Samuel 7:2). David consulted Nathan the prophet, asking approval for his plans to build a temple. But Nathan told David that, while God approved of his desire to build a temple he could not build it because the king had the blood of many battles on his hands. David's son, Solomon, was chosen instead to build the first temple in Jerusalem.

Mount Moriah, the site chosen by King David for the temple, was believed to be the very place to which, centuries earlier, Abraham had brought his son Isaac for sacrifice. Although forbidden to construct the temple, David began to gather the materials that would be needed to build the permanent place of worship. When Solomon succeeded his father, he took on the task of constructing the temple, and in about 950 B.C. dedicated the magnificent structure in which the people could worship their God (1 Kings 6–7; 2 Chronicles 3–4).

Although the temple that Solomon built was much larger than the tabernacle, it was built to the same basic floorplan and design. Just like the tabernacle, it contained a Holy Place and Holy of Holies, the ark of the covenant, the table of showbread, the seven-branched lampstand (*menorah*) and other special furniture such as the altar and laver.

Solomon's Temple stood for more than four hundred years, while the nation's fortunes continued to wax and wane. During Solomon's reign, the nation knew great prosperity; but shortly afterwards, under his son Rehoboam, things began to go wrong. The Israelites were defeated by the Egyptians, who plundered all the temple treasures, including the valuable gold vessels and utensils used in worship (1 Kings 14:25–26). These were later replaced with bronze vessels.

Finally, after four centuries of victories and defeats, Solomon's Temple was destroyed in 586 B.C. by the invading Babylonian army. The Jewish people were led away captive to Babylon, and the temple and city of Jerusalem were laid waste (2 Kings 24:10–13).

Only fifty years later the fortunes of the Jews changed yet again. The Persians seized Babylon, and the Persian king, Cyrus, encouraged the Israelites to return to their own city, Jerusalem. Not all made the return journey, but those who did began to rebuild the city and the temple under the Jewish leaders Ezra and Nehemiah. Though they did not have the wealth to build a temple as grand as Solomon's, the reconstructed building was nevertheless quite imposing. Many of "the older priests wept aloud in disappointment" at its appearance (Ezra 3:7–13). Yet this temple, as rebuilt by Zerubbabel (c. 537–15 B.C.), served as the focus of Jewish worship and sacrifice for the next few hundred years, despite difficult times when the Jews were defeated and even overrun by their enemies.

Then, in 164 B.C., under the leadership of the Maccabees, the Jews managed to regain their freedom, fighting a war of liberation against the Seleucids, whose king, Antiochus IV, had ritually polluted the temple by setting up a pagan altar there. After the Maccabean victory, the temple was cleansed and re-dedicated (1 Maccabees 4:36–59). The city of Jerusalem was partially rebuilt, and extensions were made to the temple. But this time of freedom did not last long, for the Romans under Pompey captured Jerusalem in 63 B.C., although they allowed Jewish worship to continue in the temple.

In 37 B.C., Herod became the puppet king of Israel, under the aegis of Rome. Herod, an Idumean rather than a Jew and a descendant of the hated Edomites, proposed building a new temple, the grandest that the Jews had ever seen. But Herod was widely regarded as a deceiver, and at first the Jews did not trust him sufficiently to allow him to proceed with his plans. Finally in 19 B.C.

Herod won the people over and began to rebuild the derelict temple, incorporating many fine additions of his own devising.

Though much despised, Herod was to become known as Herod the Great, as much as anything for his remarkable building projects, which also included the port of Caesarea, the strongholds of Herodion and Masada, and the city of Tiberias by the Sea of Galilee. Although Herod succeeded in building the grandest temple, it was a God-forsaken place, built to pacify the Jews and curry their favor; built to Herod's glory rather than to the glory of God.

This magnificent temple stood for less than one hundred years. Six years after its completion, in A.D. 70, it was totally destroyed by the Roman legions under Titus, who had been called in to quell the Jewish Revolt of A.D. 66–70. Herod's Temple was the last Jewish temple to stand on this sacred site in Jerusalem; although much has happened there over the last two thousand years, the Jewish temple has never been rebuilt.

The Roman occupation of Palestine lasted in all for some three hundred years. After Herod's Temple had been destroyed, the Romans occupied its site, and a Roman temple dedicated to Jupiter was possibly erected over it. It also appears that the Emperor Hadrian set up statues in the temple area.

After 325, when Christianity became tolerated throughout the Roman Empire, the Christian church grew fast and became established throughout the Mediterranean. Between A.D. 330 and 638, the Byzantine period, Jerusalem became the focus of the Christian religion, and many churches and shrines were built in the city. Little happened on the Temple Mount itself, which apparently had scant significance for contemporary Christians.

In 638, the Muslims conquered Palestine and occupied the temple site. At the center of the Temple Mount, they built in 691–2 the Dome of the Rock , as well as a mosque known as al-Aqsa, earlier, in 639–40. The Muslims firmly established their religion in Jerusalem, building various other shrines and mosques. Thus Jerusalem had now become an important holy place for the Jewish, Christian, and Muslim religions.

This first Muslim period was brought to an abrupt end in 1099 by the arrival of the Crusader armies, who, in their religious fervor and lust for booty, "liberated" the temple site and the city for Christianity—in the process massacring Muslims and any Jews they found. For a brief period in the twelfth century, the Crusaders turned the city into a predominantly Christian enclave once more, evidence of which remains in some of their splendid buildings, such as the Church of St Anne, near the ruins of the Pool of Bethesda.

However in 1187, the Crusaders were ejected from Jerusalem by the Muslim Mamluks, who held sway until 1517. The Mamluks initiated the work of rebuilding the city walls, but left little impression on the rest of the city.

In 1517, the Ottoman Turks took over from the Mamluks, holding the city until 1917 when they were defeated by the Allies during the First World War. The Turks built on a vast scale, reconstructing the walls around the city and the temple. Many of the walls of the Old City that we see today, as well as the Golden Gate and other significant buildings, were built by Suleiman the Magnificent (1520–66) at the beginning of this period. He also conserved the Temple Mount area.

Various other religious and ethnic groups had found their way to Jerusalem by the beginning of the twentieth century, including many shades of opinion among Jews, Muslims, and Christians. The British took over control from the Turks in 1917, ruling by mandate from the League of Nations from 1922. Despite all efforts to bring unity to Palestine, there was only failure. Jew, Arab, and Christian remained poles apart.

Israel was established as an independent state in 1948, against the strong opposition of the Arabs. West Jerusalem came fully under Jewish control, to which East Jerusalem was added in 1967 after the Israeli victory in the Six Day War. The Temple Mount site itself, however, is still controlled today by the Muslims, for whom it is a sacred place.

Since 1948, various excavations and explorations have been undertaken in an attempt to establish the history of the temple site. The remains of the mass of buildings on this site, if studied carefully, can help us visualize how the temple appeared in the time of Herod the Great.

The Temple Mount is today dominated by the Islamic Dome of the Rock, built on the site of Herod's Temple.

2. How We Know about Herod's Temple

There are many written sources of information about the Second Temple, as Herod's Temple is usually known. It is important that we make use of only the most reliable evidence, as many people with a particular ax to grind have written about the temple, trying to prove a particular point or to convince readers of some extreme religious view.

First of all, there is evidence from the Old and New Testaments of the Bible. This information is, in fact, quite scanty, consisting of some measurements, together with descriptions of incidents, and it is only sufficient to supplement other available information. The works of Josephus, a Jewish historian who lived during the heyday of Herod's Temple, and witnessed its destruction, are one of our major sources of information. Josephus's writings, *Jewish Antiquities* and *The Jewish War,* provide plenty of information but are, in parts, difficult to interpret and need careful sifting, as they sometimes appear to contradict other sources, most notably the Mishnah.

I believe that the Mishnah, a codification of the oral Jewish law compiled around A.D. 200, is the most valuable source of information about the Second Temple, and I have relied upon it heavily during my research. Like the Bible and Josephus, the evidence from the Mishnah is difficult to interpret, as it sometimes appears to be self-contradictory as well as inconsistent with other available information. However, with careful study, it is possible to discern chronological differences between various statements in the Mishnah. For instance, the Mishnah's description of the tabernacle gives us some valuable insights into Herod's Temple, which was built to a similar plan.

A further valuable source of evidence on the temple is Alfred Edersheim's book *The Temple: Its Ministry and Services.* Edersheim was a learned nineteenth-century Jew who adopted the Christian faith and wrote much about the temple and matters of Jewish interest. I have drawn heavily on his book, which is itself largely based upon the Mishnah. Edersheim's book is also very helpful in explaining the Mishnah, Josephus, and other sources.

Among contemporary sources, I find very helpful the work and writings of Dan Bahat, a leading archaeologist in Jerusalem—particularly his *Carta's Atlas of Jerusalem.* Dr. Leen Ritmeyer has proved another useful source, with his doctoral thesis; his many articles in the *Biblical Archaeology Review,* including an important article in the January/February 1996 issue about *Es Sakhra* (The Rock); and booklets such as *The Reconstruction of Herod's Temple Mount in Jerusalem.*

Es Sakhra is a rock situated within the Dome of the Rock and is also known as the Foundation Rock. Ritmeyer's article not only provides important evidence about this rock but also gives vital clues concerning the position of the Holy of Holies within the temple. Though not conclusive, much of the evidence cited

Floor of the Dome of the Rock
as observed by Dr. Leen Ritmeyer

(Biblical Archaeology Review Volume 22, No 1, 1996)

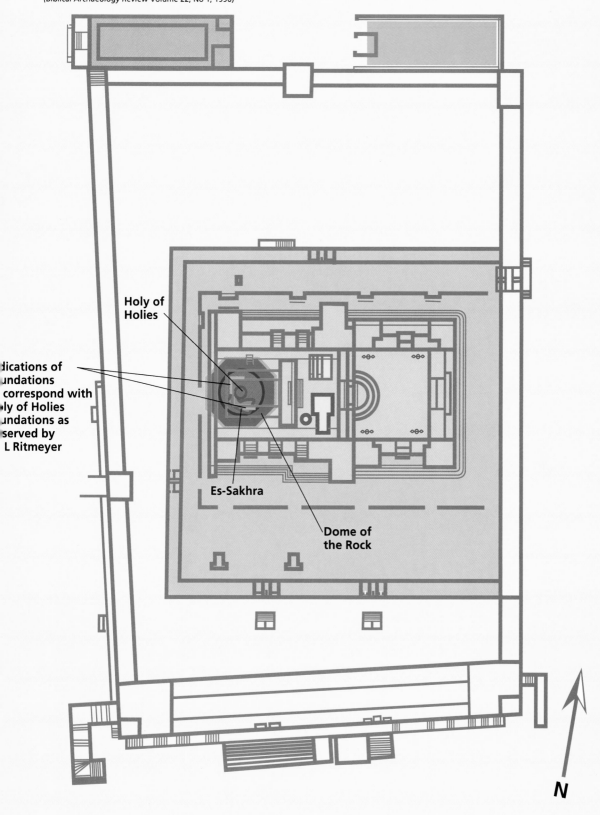

Holy of
Holies

dications of
undations
 correspond with
ly of Holies
undations as
served by
L Ritmeyer

Es-Sakhra

Dome of
the Rock

N

Robinson's Arch—discovered by the American archaeologist Edward Robinson, formed part of Herod's Temple, and is still visible in the Temple Mount platform.

agrees with the measurements for the Holy of Holies given in the Mishnah.

Es Sakhra has seen many changes over the years, particularly during the Crusades. We know that at that time—and probably in the preceding Byzantine Christian period—little importance was ascribed to this rock or to the temple itself, as they were considered to have been superseded by Christianity.

Despite many changes to the rock over the centuries, there is still evidence of "channels" running round its edge. It is difficult to examine these channels closely because of the structures that the Muslims have erected around the Dome of the Rock. But, with care, the position of these channels and of the foundations that they would have supported can be construed. Where visible, these channels correspond exactly with what I believe to have been the position of the wall of the Holy of Holies and were, I have little doubt, the excavations needed to level off the rock that supported these walls. This accords with what is written in the Mishnah.

Since the temple was destroyed in A.D. 70, almost all the masonry above the temple platform is of a later date and is either Muslim, Crusader, Christian, or Turkish. Almost everything below the platform dates to Herod's time or even earlier.

Modern archaeological interest in the temple site began in the 1850s, when a number of excavations were carried out. Enjoying more freedom of access than is currently available, archaeologists such as Edward Robinson, an American professor; J.T. Barclay, a British architect and explorer; and Charles Wilson, a British army officer; explored various parts of the temple. Another British officer, the Royal Engineer Col. Charles Warren, made charts and diagrams of the various types of masonry, their location and dating, and of the underground chambers that he found beneath the temple site.

These Victorian archaeologists' explorations, especially those of Warren, who drew up charts and diagrams for the Palestine Exploration Fund, have left us many helpful clues to the positions of various parts of the temple. Unfortunately, their excavations ceased at the beginning of the First World War.

After 1914, little further exploration took place until Israel became an independent state in 1948. Work then began again in earnest, and we are able to use evidence discovered by Yigael Yadin, Benjamin Mazar, Asher S. Kaufman, Dan Bahat, Leen Ritmeyer, and other archaeologists to visualize the temple as it was before the Roman sack of Jerusalem in A.D. 70.

3. The Stones of the Temple

As has been explained above, Herod's Temple was not a totally new complex of buildings but a grand extension and refurbishment of the earlier temple on this site, which dated back to Solomon's time, c. 950 B.C. Herod's prime aim in rebuilding the temple on such an extravagant scale was to ingratiate himself with the Jews, who viewed him with suspicion as a hated Edomite who owed his position as ruler to the occupying Roman power.

When Herod the Great set about building this far more glorious temple—to his own glory rather than to God's—his starting point was the remains of Solomon's Temple, which Zerubbabel, returning from exile in Babylon, had repaired with his limited resources and which the Hasmoneans had extended in the time of the Maccabees, c. 165–142 B.C.

So Herod inherited a five-hundred-cubit-square temple platform and its buildings, with the sanctuary—consisting of the Holy Place and Most Holy Place—at its heart. In order to fulfil his grandiose conception, Herod needed a much more extensive platform. The existing ground levels did not allow for this, however. Not only were they

Alec Garrard's model of the Temple viewed from above, to show clearly the Temple Court.

uneven but also they fell away sharply. Herod first had to fill in the many lower areas and build massive retaining walls to hold the platform in place.

The obvious way to extend such a platform would have been to build a new retaining wall and then fill in with rubble behind it. However, Herod's retaining walls, remains of which still stand, were built of such huge blocks of stone that it was quite impracticable to hoist them into place course after course. For this reason, a different technique was used. The extended platform was built up with rubble sufficient to maneuver into place from behind one course of stones at a time to form the retaining wall. The level was gradually raised, one course at a time, until it eventually matched the level of the old temple platform.

With the help of rollers, the massive stones of the retaining wall, 1.2 meters (four feet) high and from 1.2 to 7.5 meters (twenty-four feet) long, were dragged from the higher ground north of the temple where they were quarried. Thus no stone-lifting or transportation of stones on carts was necessary, if indeed feasible.

The entire enclosed area of the temple covered in all about thirty-five acres (fifteen hectares). The eastern wall was about 995 [short] cubits in length, while the five-hundred-cubit square in the center, which formed the base of Solomon's Temple, was measured in long cubits, each fifty cm (twenty inches) long. We need to remember these differing units of measurement, or we shall think the temple plan is inaccurate.

The south side, or front, of the temple was about six hundred cubits long. Now I am aware that the cubit can vary in length, making other measurements approximate. When Josephus talked of measurements in feet, he meant the Roman foot, which was different from the Imperial foot; similarly his cubit can vary from that used by the Mishnah. Few of the sizes and locations of the buildings on the temple site are known exactly, and measuring in cubits allows for some vari-

ation. We will understand the drawings and plans better if we bear in mind that they are not always drawn strictly to scale.

To the east of the temple lies the Kidron Valley, with the Mount of Olives beyond, important to the temple since key sacrifices were made there. On the western side was the Tyropoeon Valley and, beyond that, the upper part of the city, where Herod and the high priest had their palaces, and where the wealthy and important people lived.

The eastern wall was the only wall whose line was left unchanged by Herod, for the simple reason that the Kidron Valley drops away sharply outside its limits. Herod's engineers merely extended the original wall at both ends, to the north and south. The point where the Herodian extension begins is clearly visible in the present-day eastern wall as a seam in the wall's masonry, usually known as the "straight joint". South of this seam, the masonry consists of finely-dressed Herodian stone blocks with a smooth boss, while those north of the seam have a rougher, projecting boss.

Recent research by Leen Ritmeyer, based on a reexamination of the Victorian archaeologist Charles Warren's records, has also suggested where the Hasmonean extension commenced to the south. Warren described a change in the direction of the eastern wall, some seventy-eight meters (two hundred and sixty feet) north of the south-east corner. This "bend", he believed, reflects a change in the masonry deep below ground and provides one of the vital clues in locating the five-hundred-cubit-square original Temple Mount.

The southern wall was about six hundred [short] cubits long, the western wall about one thousand and forty cubits long, and the northern wall about six hundred and fifty-five cubits.

If we now concentrate on the masonry itself, inside the walls on the eastern side there are some significant stones at a lower level by the Golden Gate. Leen Ritmeyer has identified here a pair of

columns, one on each side of the gate, as originating from Solomon's Temple. If his identification is correct, they pinpoint the exact position of this gate and also the northeast corner of the five-hundred-cubit-square on which the First Temple was built.

In only one other place have traces of masonry been found which could date from as early as Solomon's time: at the northwest corner of the temple site, where today a a flight of steps leads up to the Dome of the Rock platform. The bottom "step" is not actually a step, but the top of a wall, and before the adjacent area was paved in modern times, the sides of this wall could be made out. If this is not Solomonic masonry, it is at any rate very early and marks the northwest corner of the five-hundred-cubit square of the First Temple. The distance from the Golden Gate to this corner of the platform measures five hundred long cubits.

There are also traces of masonry dating from the time of Ezra and Nehemiah in the eastern wall, and experts agree that this masonry formed part of the original temple wall. While all the masonry above the platform is later—Crusader, Byzantine, or Muslim—that lying below the platform is earlier. There are also traces of masonry from Nehemiah's time around the Golden Gate.

At the southeast corner of the eastern wall, near the slight bend noted by Charles Warren, a short stretch of masonry dates from the Hasmonean extension of the temple.

The eastern wall of the Royal Porch is also Herodian, as is the masonry along the front, or south face, of the Temple Mount, where the Double and Triple Gates and general entrances were located, and where much recent archaeological excavation has taken place. Many people believe these stones are not Herodian, although they extend below the platform. However, they are easily identifiable as Herodian by the characteristic margins round the ashlars.

All the masonry of the lower part of the western wall has been identified as

The busy southwest corner of the Temple Mount. People entered the Temple Mount from the monumental stairway leading over Robinson's Arch (*center foreground*), from the shops under the narrow street running along the Western Wall (*left*), and from the main street which ran from the Pool of Siloam in the south to the northern city gate. They also entered from the east (*right*).

The eastern wall viewed from the southeast. When Herod extended the Temple Mount platform, the line of this wall was not altered because the Kidron Valley drops away sharply, and dictates the line of the wall. (*Inset*) The eastern wall of the Old City today, showing the Dome of the Rock on the temple site.

Herodian, so we know that this wall was built in Herod's time to extend the temple. The original, pre-Herodian wall was sited further east and within the present Temple Mount area.

There are a few signs of Herodian masonry at the site of the Roman Antonia Fortress, on the northwest corner of the Temple Mount. The Antonia Fortress, named after Mark Antony, was built on a rock that stood higher than the original temple platform. We assume that Herod had this rock leveled and its sides squared off to increase its defensibility. Josephus's description proves it was a very difficult place to storm, and so it formed a solid, impregnable fortification. Though later buildings now stand around this rock, it still can be identified and marks precisely the location of the Antonia Fortress.

The measurements we can make today do not match exactly Josephus's records. However, the original defensive tower, called the Tower of Baris, stood further in on the northwest corner of the five-hundred-cubit square. Using this evidence, we can measure from several established points and identify some of the descriptions in Josephus or the Mishnah.

All the buildings on the Temple Mount and within the Temple Court were demolished by the Romans, so there are no remains to indicate the location or appearance of the temple sanctuary and the buildings surrounding it; all we have to go on are the descriptions in Josephus's writings and in the Mishnah. However, the platform on which the Muslim Dome of the Rock is built must have been part of the original platform of the Jewish temple, since it would have been extremely laborious, not to say pointless, to remove it. So we may conclude that the level of the platform today corresponds roughly with the level and location of the Herodian Temple platform.

Inside the Dome of the Rock is located what is known as *Es-Sakhra*, the Foundation Stone. If we look closely at it, we can see that at different times it has been cut and shaped. We can be fairly certain that this was the rock within the Holy of Holies on which the high priest sprinkled the bulls' and goats' blood once a year, on the Day of Atonement, since its height corresponds roughly with the measurements given in the Mishnah. We do not know what has happened to it in the intervening years, or how high it once was; but as the temple was burned by he Romans, it is likely that the limestone ock was damaged by the heat of the fire.

The temple complex was originally ntered through a number of gates. The isitor climbed impressive flights of steps utside the wall and ascended further teps inside the temple complex to enter he Court of the Gentiles, which was pen to all classes of visitor.

As the visitor approached the sanctury, he or she next reached the 1.4 meter 4 foot 6 inch) "Wall of Partition." This vas punctuated with a number of openngs, through which only Jews could ass into the Court of Israel, while Gentiles were forbidden to go any furher on pain of death.

The next stage, from holy ground to holier ground, lay through the Court of he Women, which marked the closest that vomen could approach the Holy Place. Although Jewish men and women could oth climb the fifteen Steps of Ascent to he platform to present their sacrifices, nly the men could proceed from that oint into the Court of the Men, or Court f the Israelites. The Court of Israel, for all ews, was outside the Temple Court, while he Court of the Israelites, for men only, vas inside the Temple Court.

Finally, at the center, came the sanctury, comprising the Holy Place and the Most Holy Place, or Holy of Holies. This vas where the priests, representing the vhole Jewish people, met God, worhiped him, and pleaded for his mercy nd forgiveness.

All the temple courtyards were surounded by porticoes, or colonnades, vhich provided shelter from the fierce heat of the sun, and, less often, from the ain. They also served as meeting-places or visitors and a market for the many commodities that the worshipers, many f whom had come long distances, needed in order to make their sacrifices. This market was solely for items for sacifice. There was an ordinary, secular market outside the temple complex for clothes, food, and other necessities.

Outside the northwest corner of the

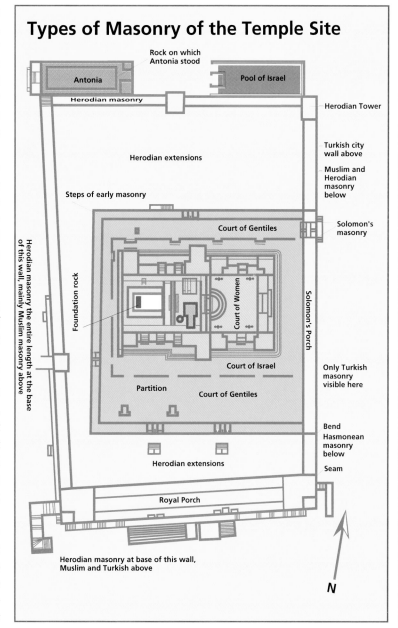

Types of Masonry of the Temple Site

Rock on which Antonia stood

Antonia

Pool of Israel

Herodian masonry

Herodian Tower

Herodian extensions

Turkish city wall above

Muslim and Herodian masonry below

Steps of early masonry

Court of Gentiles

Solomon's masonry

Herodian masonry the entire length at the base of this wall, mainly Muslim masonry above

Foundation rock

Court of Women

Solomon's Porch

Court of Israel

Only Turkish masonry visible here

Partition

Court of Gentiles

Bend Hasmonean masonry below

Seam

Herodian extensions

Royal Porch

Herodian masonry at base of this wall, Muslim and Turkish above

N

temple stood the Roman fortress of Antonia, which housed the Roman garrison. It kept watch over the temple, constantly ready to restore order if required.

Beneath the temple site, cut in the easily quarried limestone, was a network of passages and chambers that provided easy and secret access between various parts of the temple, and also formed cisterns that stored winter rain for the temple's water requirements through the long dry season. Water was also brought in by aqueduct from Solomon's Pools, situated some miles south of Jerusalem.

4. The Outer Gates of the Temple

'The LORD loves the Gates of Zion' (Psalm 87:2)

Following the overview in the previous chapter, we will now consider each part of the temple in detail. Tracing the imaginary footsteps of a first-century Jewish worshiper, we will make our way from the outer gates right into the sanctuary, each stage we reach holier than the last.

The gates of the temple were, for the most part, much more than doors. They consisted of two- or three-story structures, with several rooms; and every gate was guarded, some more strictly than others. Most of the gates that led into the temple precincts from outside had, as far as we know, no official names. They have simply been named after their location or after the archaeologist who discovered them. There was one external gate on the eastern side of the Temple Mount platform, two on the south, four on the west, and one on the north.

The sole external gate on the eastern side is usually known as the eastern gate, but it is also called the Gate of the Palace of Shushan, or the Shushan Gate. This gate gave direct access to the outer temple courts and formed part of the five-hundred-cubit-square original temple area.

This important gate has been located and identified by Ritmeyer from some masonry found beneath the present Golden Gate. It stood at the corner of the Temple Mount and looked straight out across the Kidron Valley to the Mount of Olives and was in precisely the same position as the equivalent gate in Solomon's Temple. (This gate has sometimes been confused with the Nicanor Gate, the principal eastern gate within the temple precincts, situated between the Court of the Women and the Court of the Priests.) On the Day of Atonement the scapegoat was taken out through the Shushan Gate and sent off over the Mount of Olives into the wilderness, symbolically carrying the sins of the people with it (Leviticus 16:6–10).

It was through the Shushan Gate, too, that the ashes from the burnt sacrifices in the temple were taken to be placed on a sacred spot on the Mount of Olives known as the Place of the Ashes. Anything that touched the altar became holy, so the altar ashes had special significance, particularly so in the case of the ashes of the two bulls that were sacrificed on the Day of Atonement. In addition to these ashes, carcasses and other remains of the burnt offerings were brought out through the Shushan Gate for final burning at the Place of the Ashes. It is not widely known that this place existed, nor is it known exactly where it was located—though it was certainly not at the pit where the red heifer was slaughtered and burnt.

Every fifty or sixty years it was necessary to sacrifice a red heifer on the Mount of Olives (see Numbers 19). We know of no more than twelve such sacrifices during the history of ancient Israel. The selected heifer was taken out through the Shushan Gate and led over a temporary wooden bridge constructed on top of the existing, permanent bridge across the Kidron valley. When the high priest sacrificed the red heifer on the Mount of Olives, he looked straight

Left: **The Double Gate in the southern wall, with the magnificent staircase leading up to it. People entered by the righthand gate, and departed via the lefthand gate.**

Below: **Interior view of the domed passageway leading from the Double Gate northwards into the temple's outer courts. The stone-carved domes contrast with the plain Double Gate.**

Bottom: **The Triple Gate, the entrance used by the priests when they came to serve in the temple.**

across the valley into the temple, over the top of the Gate of the Pure and Just and through the Nicanor Gate. He did not look through the Shushan Gate, as some believe, since the latter was not in a direct line with the temple and was at a lower level than the other two gates. Wherever the high priest was standing on the Mount of Olives when he sacrificed the red heifer, he could not possibly have seen through the Shushan Gate into the temple sanctuary.

Another matter confuses many people about the Shushan Gate. We read in Ezekiel that the eastern gate is bricked up and will only be opened when the Prince comes to enter it. But this prophecy does not refer to the Golden Gate, which stands today over the site of the Shushan Gate and is a Muslim gate built in the fifteenth century. The Golden Gate was bricked up when the temple area was sealed; because it is blocked up, it is often claimed that Ezekiel was referring to this gate. But if we read Ezekiel 46:2–8 in *The New International Version*, we realize that these prophecies refer to the inner eastern Gate, through which sacrifices were taken to be received by the priests. The only people allowed through this gate in Ezekiel's time were priests; but it was going to be opened up for all to enter.

Overall view of the temple model from the southeast corner.

The Eastern, or Shushan, Gate, which led directly from the Kidron Valley and the Mount of Olives into the temple courts. The Mishnah says that the gate featured a representation of the Palace of Shushan in Babylon.

Many people say that Jesus entered the Shushan Gate in triumph on Palm Sunday, when he went into the Temple Court and overturned the money-changers' tables (Matthew 21:10–12). However the money-changers' tables were not located here, but by the Hulda Gate on the southern side of the temple. Matthew states that Jesus entered the *city*; but the Shushan Gate led straight from the Mount of Olives into the *temple*. If Jesus entered the city directly from the Mount of Olives, he must have entered by another gate.

Although we believe, following the Gospels, that people of Jesus' time entered the temple precincts through the Shushan Gate, they were actually using this route in contravention of the regulations, as a short-cut into Jerusalem. It was possible to enter by this gate and leave again by the Coponius Gate, thereby gaining direct access to the main part of the city and saving a circuitous two-mile walk. But this was not an offi-

cial entrance, only an exit used during a number of specific temple ceremonies and sacrifices. The Mishnah states that people had to go through a special procedure to enter here.

Near the southeast corner of the temple site were two small entrances—doors rather than gates—through which supplies for running the temple were taken in for storage in the extensive chambers located under the Royal Porch. These two small entrances are not mentioned in the written sources, but traces of them can still be seen in the wall today, as well as traces of stairs leading up to them.

In front of the southern wall of the temple area, which was the main approach to the temple, was a large open space where people congregated, with shops, baths, and administrative buildings. The most easterly gate in this wall was the Triple Gate, reached via a grand fifteen-meter-wide (fifty foot) staircase. This gate was completely demolished when the temple was destroyed, so the present so-called "Triple Gate" is not original.

The original Triple Gate was the entrance used by the priests when they came to serve in the temple, and a passageway gave direct access into the inner temple court. From the evidence discovered on diagrams on tools found during excavations in Jerusalem, we believe the Triple Gate comprised a large central gate, with a smaller gate on each side. The Triple Gate led into a large and elaborate chamber, with columns and decorated ceilings, and seems to have connected directly with the vaulted store-rooms under the Royal Porch in the southeast part of the temple platform, where materials needed for the temple services were housed.

A tomb complex of this same period in the nearby Hinnom Valley, identified as belonging to the high priestly family of Annas, reinforces the view that this gate was used by the priests. The architectural style of these tombs was very similar to that of Herod's Temple, and

Wilson's Gate, a large and elaborate entrance to the Western Porch, named after the archaeologist who discovered the remains of the arch which supported the approach to it.

the central tomb has a triple opening apparently modeled on the Triple Gate of the temple, which was clearly visible from this part of the Hinnom Valley. The priests for whom this tomb was built seemingly wanted their place of rest to be a miniature replica of the magnificent gate that they used during their priestly duties. Unfortunately, little is left of the original Triple Gate, so we can piece together only these scraps of evidence in our attempt to visualize its appearance.

The other gate in the southern wall is the Double Gate. The Double and Triple Gates have often been confused with the Hulda Gates; but while the former were external gates, the Hulda Gates were inner entrances, within the original five-hundred-cubit square. *Middot* 1.3 speaks of "the two Hulda Gates on the south that served for coming in and going out," and it is this statement that has led many scholars to identify the Double and Triple Gates with the Hulda Gates. But we must remember that *Middot* restricts its description of Herod's Temple to the area of the *pre-Herodian* Temple Mount. The southern wall of the original five-hundred-cubit-square platform had two

gates, known as the Hulda Gates, each with two openings. Later, in the Herodian period, a long passageway was built to link the original Hulda Gates with the new, outer, Double Gate in the southern wall.

The new Double Gate to Herod's Temple was the main public entrance to the Temple Mount, approached by an impressive sixty-four-meter-wide (210 foot) staircase leading up from the Lower City. The staircase consisted of thirty steps, laid alternately as steps and landings, planned to encourage worshipers to climb them slowly and reverently. The Double Gate was formed of two huge gates, with people entering through the eastern, righthand gateway, and exiting through the western, lefthand gateway. The Double Gate led into a major passageway under the Royal Porch, which then opened out into the courtyard just in front of the Hulda Gates. Herod developed new building techniques when he rebuilt the Double Gate, and although his first experiment collapsed, the second succeeded.

Devoid of ornament outside, the Double Gates were each surmounted by a massive lintel and relieving arch. By

Interior of Wilson's Arch, which supported the bridge spanning the Tyropoeon Valley and connecting the western part of Jerusalem to the Temple Mount. Today the arch forms part of the Western Wall complex.

contrast, the passageways inside displayed superb Herodian masonry and intricate stone-carving. This Double Gate—and not the Gate of the Pure and the Just as so many people think—is the "Beautiful Gate" where the apostles Peter and John encountered the crippled man (Acts 3:2). Its beauty was not so much in its external appearance as in the decorated ceiling within the passageway. Though today concealed from the outside by additions dating from the Early Islamic and Crusader periods, entering from inside the Temple Mount one finds these gates and a large part of the passageways amazingly intact. Anyone who can distinguish different types of masonry and periods of building can see exactly where the Double Gate was and what it looked like.

Inside the Double Gate, long passageways, roofed with domes supported on columns, rose to the north to give access to the outer courts of the temple. These domes are unique, the earliest surviving examples of shallow spherical domes with continuous spherical pendentives. Four of the six surviving domes display the unique stone-carved decoration that the Herodian craftsmen adapted from Roman decorative styles to conform to Jewish law, using no figurative representation. Instead they featured elaborate geometrical and floral motifs, proliferating with vines and acanthus leaves.

We come next to the Western, or Wailing, Wall. As we have noticed previously, each of the gates in the Western Wall is named after the archaeologist who discovered it; we do not know whether the gates originally had official names.

From the south, the first of these gates, known as Robinson's Arch, was the main entrance into the Royal Porch, or Stoa. A monumental stairway led over Robinson's Arch, which stood some twenty-four meters (eighty feet) high, and into the Royal Stoa, or Basilica, which ran the whole length of the southern wall. Only fit, healthy people could climb right up to this gate. In *Antiquities* 15.412, Josephus describes the magnificent Royal Porch as "a structure more noteworthy than any under the sun. For where the depth of the ravine was great ... the height of the portico standing over it was so very great that if anyone looked down from its rooftop he would become dizzy and his vision would be unable to reach the end of so measureless a depth."

The next gate along the Western Wall is Barclay's Gate—one of two low-level

The Temple Gates

1. Entrance to Temple
2. Entrance to Porch
3. Nicanor Gate (Eastern Gate)
4. Gate of the Pure and Just
5. Shushan Gate (Eastern Gate)
6. Water Gate
7. Gate of the Firstborn
8. Gate of the Wood
9. Gate of the Flame
10. Sacrifice Gate
11. Beth-Moked Gate (side gate)
12. Beth-Moked Gate (main gate)
13. Gate of the Music
14. Gate of the Women—general entrance
15. Hulda Gate—priests

16. Hulda Gate—people
17. Coponius Gate
18. Tadi Gate
19. Triple Gate
20. Double Gate
21. Robinson's Arch (Western Gate)
22. Barclay's Gate
23. Wilson's Arch (Gate)
24. Warren's Gate
25. Northern Gate
26. Antonia Gate
27. Priest's Gate

1A. Side gates to Temple entrance
3A. Side gates to Eastern Gate

The Temple Gates

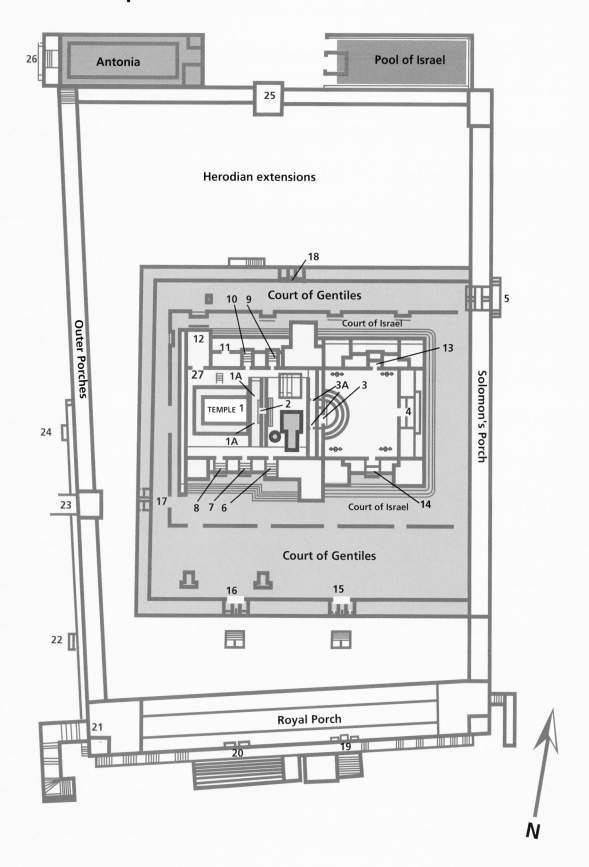

Antonia

Pool of Israel

26

25

Herodian extensions

18

Court of Gentiles

5

10 9

Court of Israel

12

11

13

27   1A

3A   3

TEMPLE 1   2

4

1A

17

8 7 6

Court of Israel

14

Outer Porches

Solomon's Porch

24

23

22

Court of Gentiles

16

15

Royal Porch

21

20   19

N

gates in this wall—named after the British architect who discovered it in 1848. Barclay's Gate has been excavated quite recently, so we know more clearly what it looked like. This entrance through Barclay's Gate led beneath the wall, turning south (to the right) as it went, and coming up via an internal staircase, illuminated when necessary, to the outer courtyard. This gate was probably used for taking in supplies for running the temple.

An external staircase also led up from Barclay's Gate to a narrow street running along the top of the Western Wall, with shops located beneath it. The remains of Barclay's Gate can still be seen today near the women's section of the Western Wall plaza, where almost half of the massive gateway lintel (eight meters (twenty-seven feet) long and two meters (seven feet) high) and the top three ashlars of its northern gatepost are preserved.

Wilson's Gate, a large and elaborate entrance to the Western Porch, was the second of the two high-level gates in the Western Wall. It is often referred to as Wilson's Arch, because remnants are still visible of the arch that supported a bridge, across which wealthy people made their way from the city into the temple.

Further north, again along the Western Wall, we come to Warren's Gate, which has been excavated along the Dan Bahat tunnel, named for the Israeli archaeologist. Warren's Gate leads off to the right, up this tunnel, into and under the temple, but it has not as yet been fully excavated. There are several theories as to its function and where it leads. Many scholars have concluded that it leads in and up under the temple, just like Barclay's

Gate. Unfortunately modern excavations of this area were stopped because the Muslims who control the site were unhappy about such work.

The Western Wall was built on a slope, and many of its stones were quarried from here, leaving a huge space. What exactly is under this site, and where the gate leads, we simply do not know. Having considered what the Mishnah tells us, and information received from Orthodox Jews, archaeologists who have worked on the site, and others (some of whose exaggerated claims cannot be taken seriously), I believe that Warren's Gate leads further than Barclay's Gate and perhaps into the holiest part of the temple.

At the northwest corner of the Temple Mount stood the Antonia Fortress, which was not, of course, part of the temple. We will discuss the various entrances to this fortress below.

On the northern side of the Temple Mount we come to the northern Gate, which many people confuse with the inner, Tadi Gate. It does not match the Mishnah's description of the Tadi and, in any case, could not have been the Tadi Gate, because it is in the outer area of the temple. This northern Gate was a general entrance for all approaching from the north, and supplies and sacrifices were brought in here too.

Just outside the northern Gate, and to the east, was a large pool or reservoir, known as the Sheep Pool, or Pool of Israel, where animals were washed before being taken into the temple for sacrifice. Every animal had to be clean—not merely for reasons of hygiene, but ritually clean, and perfect in every way—before it could be slaughtered.

5. The Temple Courtyards

"Enter . . . his courts with praise" (Psalm 100:4)

The temple area comprised a number of courtyards: the Outer Courtyard, composed of extensions added to the original temple square at various times; and, within the Outer Courtyard, the Court of the Gentiles, the Court of the Women, and the Court of the Priests. Each courtyard possessed a different degree of holiness, culminating in the holiest at the center. Only ritually clean Jewish worshipers were allowed to enter the inner courtyards.

The Mishnaic tractate *Kelim* 1.6–9 describes the areas that surrounded the temple in ascending degrees of holiness. Outside the temple was the land of Israel itself, then the city of Jerusalem, then the original square Temple Mount of Solomon's time and the rampart (*hel* in Hebrew), the low terrace that bounded the wall of the temple. Next, still moving inwards, came the Court of the Women (a large court with four huge lampstands), the Court of the Israelites, and the Court of the Priests, where the priests performed the temple services. The area between the sanctuary porch and the altar was next in ascending order of holiness, followed by the sanctuary, until, finally, the innermost part of the temple—known literally as the Holiest Place, or the Holy of Holies—was reached.

As we have seen, the temple was a vast building for its period, covering some thirty-five acres (fourteen hectares)—about one fifth of the area of the city of Jerusalem—with huge retaining walls built around its periphery to support the flat platform on which it was built.

Within the southern wall of the temple was the Royal Porch, or Royal Stoa,

Immediately outside the Southern Wall of the Temple Mount was a busy market where cloth, wool, shoes, dates, and other foodstuffs were sold.

a very grand structure, the largest single building on the temple site (see below, chapter 7). Outside the Royal Porch was a large open space from which people approached the temple, whose huge outer wall towered above them. To the south lay the old City of David and the Pool of Siloam. This open space was a busy marketplace where visitors and Jerusalemites met and replenished their stores. As we have seen, an impressive 120-cubit-wide staircase of thirty steps led up from this area to the Double Gate, the main public entrance to the temple.

Between the Triple and Double Gates, standing just a short distance from the south wall, was a small building for the use of those who wanted to take a sacred bath before entering the temple. A second building was used for administration and also for sittings of one of the Jewish lower courts.

The sophisticated Jewish legal system was divided into the Lower, Middle, and Higher Courts, called respectively the First Gate, Middle Gate, and Last Gate. According to the Mishnah, the Lower Court was presided over by three, five, seven, or even nine judges and was for petty sessions. The Middle Court was presided over by twenty-three judges and was for more serious offences. In some respects, it was similar to an English County Court today. The Higher Court, known as the Sanhedrin, was presided over by seventy-one judges—or seventy and one, as the Mishnah says—and was the supreme court. The court building in front of the south wall of the temple was for trying only minor cases and deciding such matters as the selection of men for temple office.

Narrow stepped streets ran along the western and southern walls of the Temple Mount. Shops selling a variety of goods were located beneath these streets. Josephus describes the battles that took place in these markets during the Jewish Revolt (*War* 2.305, 315, 339). He also describes the timber market (*War* 2.530) and a district that contained "wool shops, braziers' smithies and the clothes market" (*War* 5. 331). In the market at the southern wall, cloth, wool, shoes, dates, and other foodstuffs were offered for sale. Caravans of camels were used to transport many of these goods to Jerusalem from distant parts.

The Outer Courtyard itself did not form part of the earlier temple square but was constructed gradually at different times. While the earlier temple site was five hundred cubits square, the Outer Courtyard was not exactly square nor were its corners precise right angles, possibly because the terrain prohibited this. However, the Outer Courtyard is always referred to as part of the temple because it and the surrounding buildings played a significant part in the life of the temple.

All the Outer Courtyard areas of the temple, including the Herodian extensions, were surrounded by porches, or colonnades, standing twenty cubits high and thirty cubits wide, and constructed of columns supporting decorated wooden roofs. The porches running round the western, northern, and eastern sides each consisted of three rows of columns, with towers at each corner, and provided worshipers with shelter from the sun and cold winds. Coming with friends to celebrate and offer sacrifices, pilgrims could walk, talk, and rest here or worship and eat sacrificial meals together. The porches rose in height where gates into the original temple square were located.

The Outer Courtyard, open for all to enter, surrounded the original Temple Mount square, the inner part of the temple complex, on its south, west, and north sides; there was no outer court on the east side.

In every major city in the Roman Empire there was a forum, or public meeting place, where business was transacted. The forum consisted of a basilica or royal porch—a large hall where people came together to do business—and an adjoining area with markets for trade

nd business. The large southern court-yard of the temple served many of the functions of a Roman forum.

In the Outer Courtyard of the temple were the so-called booths, or stalls, of Annas, a man who exercised tight con-rol over the priesthood in Herod's Temple. These stalls sold a variety of goods that people could buy to give as sacrificial offerings in the temple, rang-ng from bulls and sheep to doves, flour, oil, wine, and wood. Since this courtyard was outside the original temple area, this did not infringe the Law of Moses or the sacred laws of the temple. There was also a well here from which people could draw water, although this water was not free. Like almost everything else in the temple, there was a charge for it.

A narrow passage between the origi-nal Temple Mount square and the outer western wall led to the northern area of this Outer Courtyard. This was the most extensive area of the Outer Courtyard added by Herod, and a variety of activi-ties went on here. As elsewhere, the porches round the outside of the north-rn Outer Courtyard were designed for people to congregate and find shelter; we read that some people even slept here. This courtyard was outside the original Temple Mount area, and the gates were not locked at night, so peo-ple were free to stay and sleep.

Also in this northern courtyard were catchment pens for sheep and bulls; when the main festivals were held, peo-ple would come here to buy their sacri-fices. This large public area was open to everybody, and people could also come here to eat their sacrifices after they had been ritually offered. The Mishnah says that people could make fires here to roast or boil their food.

In the northwest corner of the north-ern Outer Courtyard was the Antonia Fortress, where a Roman garrison was stationed. The soldiers were often drilled and paraded in the northern Outer Courtyard in an attempt to overawe and intimidate the Jewish people. A staircase in the northwest corner of the courtyard gave access to the Antonia Fortress, lead-ing into another courtyard used by the administration of the fortress.

There were entrances on three sides from the Outer Courtyard to the earlier Temple Mount square: the two Hulda Gates on the south side; the Coponius Gate on the west side; the Tadi Gate on the north side; while on the east side, the Eastern Gate, or Gate of Shushan, led directly into the Kidron Valley.

Immediately surrounding these gates was the Court of the Gentiles, which all could enter, as was the case with the Outer Courtyard—though more controls were imposed here, as it was within the true temple area. It was here that Jesus overthrew the tables, which were contravening the Law since they were *within* the sacred part of the temple.

The Court of the Gentiles was surrounded by a porch or colonnade, smaller than the colonnades in the Outer Courtyard, but nevertheless a place where people met, found shelter, and sometimes ate and rested. Guards posted all the way around kept a strict eye on everything that went on, to ensure that the temple regulations were not violated.

On the southern side of the Court of the Gentiles, just inside the Hulda Gates, were situated underground chambers where people could take a sacred bath, which was compulsory for all who entered the temple court. Worshipers had to immerse themselves completely to be made ritually clean. There were two bathing chambers, one for men, the other for women, and also a well from which water could be drawn for drinking, washing, and cooking.

Many people consider that the Court of the Gentiles was identical with the Outer Courtyard area described above. But the Mishnah, without naming the Court of the Gentiles, describes the Hulda Gates as the outer porch and says that *after* entering the Hulda Gates one came to the partition, with openings in it guarded by the priests, through which Gentiles were forbidden to pass on pain of death. The Mishnah says this partition was within the Temple Mount itself, so the Court of the Gentiles, too, must have been within the Temple Mount.

Josephus mentions the Court of the Gentiles and describes the route from the Royal Porch to the temple; however, he does not mention the porches round the Temple Mount square, only the partition that surrounds the temple. I conclude that the Court of the Gentiles was within the Temple Mount square, and that the Court of Israel was within the partition prohibited to Gentiles, though we do not know the precise position of this partition.

Josephus also tells us that the Roman soldiers invading the temple during the Jewish Revolt were held off at this point for some considerable time. If the Court of the Gentiles was surrounded merely by a partition, as some writers suggest, this would surely not have been sufficient barrier for the defenders to have held off the Roman army for long; so there must have been some more substantial barrier here, such as a porch or wall. For this reason, I conclude that the five-hundred-cubit original Temple Mount square was probably surrounded by a substantial porch.

Moving further inwards, we come to the Court of Prayer, often called the Court of the Women, not because it was reserved exclusively for women's worship, but because women could not go beyond this point. This court was considered to be more holy than the Outer Courtyard, and worshipers came here to meet the priests at the hour of prayer bringing with them their sacrifices. The priest stood on a platform and addressed the worshipers as they gathered in the morning or during the day. The laypeople entered the Court of Prayer by the gate on the south, sometimes called the Womens Gate, climbing three steps and crossing a platform. If they were people of importance, they entered by the gate on the east side, the Gate of the Pure and the Just.

Some time after the completion of the Court of the Women, balconies were built on three sides of the court so that women could worship above, and men below as they were to be segregated during worship (*Middot* 2.5, *Sukkah* 5.2). Porches, or porticoes, ran around the Court of Prayer, as they did around the other courtyards; but this porch was more important as senior rabbis taught here

Less qualified rabbis preached in Solomon's Porch, or even right outside the Temple Mount area. According to the Bible, Jesus preached in the Court of Prayer at the end of his ministry.

Within the Court of Prayer stood thirteen collection boxes, to which people brought their contributions for the temple. Such gifts were made as freewill offerings, over and above the tithes and other compulsory offerings, such as temple tribute.

Inside the porch of the Court of Prayer, and generally located on its west side, were the fifteen Steps of Ascent, where people brought their sacrifices and offerings to the priest. On special occasions, such as religious festivals, the priests stood on a platform at the top of these fifteen steps and addressed the people standing at the Eastern Gate.

Within the Court of Prayer stood four giant lampstands, which were lit on special occasions. At these times, the temple gates were left open all night, so that the people could gather and celebrate. There was also a platform where musi-

cians played their instruments. Normally the Levites sang and played here; but at times of special rejoicing, everyone joined in.

The Mishnah says that the Court of Prayer was originally completely open, but walls were later built around it, with chambers added at its four corners, as well as porches and lamps.

Moving further in again, we come finally to the Court of the Priests, the holiest of all the courts, which only the priests could enter. The temple sanctuary itself stood at the center of this court, with other buildings and porches surrounding it.

Three entrances led into the Court of Priests from the terrace to the south: the Wood Gate, the Gate of the Firstborn, and the Water Gate. There were three further entrances to the Court of the Priests on its north side: the Gate of the Chamber of the Hearth, where the priests lived; the Sacrifice Gate, through which the sacrifices were brought; and the Gate of the Flame, over which the eternal flame burned. On the east side of the Court of the Priests stood the Eastern, or

A bird's-eye view of the Court of the Women, so called because it was the furthest that women were permitted to progress into the temple precincts. The four great lampstands are clearly visible, as is the inner eastern gate, with its semicircular staircase.

The sanctuary and courts of the temple viewed from the northeast.

One of the magnificent golden lampstands which stood in the Court of the Women, which was featured particularly in the annual Feast of Tabernacles, or Succoth.

Nicanor, Gate, opening from the Court of Prayer.

A special area within the Court of the Priests was reserved for Jewish men who were bringing sacrifices, making offerings, or meeting priests. The remainder of the Court of the Priests, the innermost court, and the smallest and holiest of all the courts, was reserved for the priests to make their sacrifices and offerings, and carry out ceremonies. Here, in front of the temple sanctuary, stood the altar of the burnt offering, upon which the offerings were placed, the blood was sprinkled, and the fires burned. Between the temple and the altar, to the south, stood the bronze laver, containing water for the priests to wash and for other sacred uses. North of the altar was the place of slaughter (*Tamid* 3.5; *Middot* 3.5), together with marble tables on which the creatures were later butchered. There were twenty-four rings here, into which the heads of the sacrificial animals were placed. After they had been killed, their carcasses were hung up in the Shambles, which consisted of eight short pillars upon which blocks of cedarwood were fastened, and into which iron hooks were fixed. On these iron hooks the carcasses were hung.

From the Court of the Priests, twelve steps led up to the temple sanctuary itself. These steps were divided into sections—three steps, then a platform, followed by another three steps, and so on until the top was reached. Only the priests were allowed to climb these steps

On the north side of the Court of the Priests, a staircase led down to an underground chamber that housed sacred baths exclusive to the priests. If any priest became ritually unclean while carrying out his duties, he could wash here and then quickly return to his post.

6. The Royal Portico

The Royal Portico, Porch, or Stoa, so called after its regal appearance rather than for any royal connection, stood high above the southern part of the temple. Josephus records that it was supported by 162 pillars, each measuring fifteen meters (fifty feet) in height and some five meters (sixteen feet) in circumference. The Royal Porch ran most of the length of the southern outer wall, with additional buildings at each end, and was probably 180 meters (600 feet/400 cubits) long and 30 meters (100 feet/64 cubits) wide. (The length is calculated from the number of pillars and the distances between them.)

Like other contemporary Roman stoa, the Royal Porch was built with two stories, and a clerestory, or raised roof with windows, on top. The capitals of the columns were "ornamented in the Corinthian style of carving, which caused amazement by the magnificence of its whole effect" (Josephus, *Antiquities* 15.414). Many fragments from the Corinthian capitals, such as acanthus leaves, volutes, and rope moldings, have been discovered during excavations. The many fragments of rosettes also found give a clue as to the style of decoration of the architrave that rested on these capitals. The second story of the Royal Porch was probably executed in the Ionic style, as fragments of columns of this architectural order have been found.

A single central walkway, thirty cubits

Interior view of the Royal Portico, or Stoa, which Herod seems to have modelled on the basilicas found throughout the Roman Empire.

The semicircular hall at the east end of the Royal Portico where the seventy-one members of the Sanhedrin sat in judgment.

kept ready for sacrifice, nor were the money-changers' tables overturned here by Jesus (Matthew 21:12,13 and Mark 11:15–17)—those tables were used for changing ordinary money into temple money to pay the temple tax.

The Royal Porch was, in effect, a basilica, used as a meeting place and market; after Herod extended the temple, it also served as the meeting place for the Sanhedrin, or Jewish supreme legislative, religious, and judicial court. Although the Sanhedrin had previously met elsewhere, around A.D. 30 it moved to the "stores" (Hebrew *hannuyot*), the name by which this elegant basilica was known, alluding to its commercial activities.

The Sanhedrin met in a semicircular structure at the east end of the Royal Porch, its seventy-one members sitting in two semicircular rows of benches, their president at the center. A massive, lavishly decorated arch stone found in the debris just outside the southern wall of the modern Temple Mount area gives an indication of the splendor of the setting of these legal sessions.

The proceedings of the Court of the Sanhedrin were open to the public and operated something like many present-day legal systems, with the decision voted on following discussion. This contrasted with a Roman judgement hall, which had closed doors and no public participation. Any decision emanating from a Roman court was made by the Roman official in charge and then announced by him, as when Pilate came out to announce his verdict on Jesus of Nazareth to the people of Jerusalem. The court in the Royal Porch, however, was open on its north side, so people could stand and watch the Sanhedrin in progress.

Although the Jewish Higher Court of the Sanhedrin and other courts were presided over by Jewish officials, whatever went on in this building was finally under Roman control. Any major decisions on affairs of state, that is, involv-

wide, ran the full length of the Royal Porch and rose to the full height of the building; two smaller walkways, each twenty cubits wide, ran parallel to, and on each side of, the central walkway. There were 162 pillars in four rows, each column fifteen meters (fifty feet) high, and with a huge circumference such that it took three men, with arms outstretched, to encircle a column.

This was a public building where people could meet and trade—serving a function rather like the House of Representatives, Stock Exchange, and Supreme Court rolled into one. Moneylenders, moneychangers, and traders also carried out their business here.

Contrary to many writers' belief, it was not in the Royal Porch that sheep were ng civil law, needed the approval of the Roman government.

The building at the east end of the Royal Porch probably housed members of the Court of the Sanhedrin, such as clerks who recorded the proceedings, and everything necessary to carry out the court's activities.

At the west end of the Royal Porch was another structure, which probably formed a large gallery and entrance. There was another entrance on the west side, approached by the huge monumental staircase that led into the Royal Porch. In the southwest corner of this building, at the end of the Royal Porch, a spiral staircase led from the basement to the top, opening onto each floor on its way up. The top of this building formed what was known as the Pinnacle of the Temple and the Place of Trumpeting.

A similar staircase at the southeast corner also climbed right to the top, with access to every floor and apartment in the building. Edersheim claimed that this was where the temptation of Jesus must have taken place, as it provided the longest drop to the ground—a distance he gives as one hundred and fifty meters (five hundred feet), including the depth of the Kidron Valley. But modern archaeological excavations have shown that a paved courtyard was located beneath this corner, so the drop would have been much shorter than Edersheim suggested.

I believe that this particular temptation of Jesus took place at the other corner, at the Place of Trumpeting, as it was here that public announcements were made. The whole point of this temptation was to announce something to the people and draw their attention to it.

Josephus described this Place of Trumpeting above the roof of the Royal Porch. One of the priests sounded a ram's horn trumpet here to herald the beginning and end of the Sabbath (*War* 4.582). One of recent excavations' prize finds was a 2.4-meter-long (8 feet) stone block that clearly fell from the parapet at this southwest corner. Tooled on three of its

Above: **The southwest corner of the Royal Portico, showing clearly the tower designated as the Place of Trumpeting.**

Left: **Bird's-eye view of the Place of Trumpeting, showing one of the priests heralding the beginning of the Sabbath.**

The inscription reading in Hebrew "to the place of trumpeting . . . " found near the southwest corner of the Temple Mount. It almost certainly comes from the tower where the priest stood to blow the *shofar* (trumpet) to announce the beginning of the Sabbath.

sides, it contained the major part of a Hebrew inscription, which can be vocalized *"L'bet hatqia l'hak . . ."*, meaning "to the place of trumpeting to . . ."—with the last, incomplete, word being open to various interpretations: most likely *l'hakriz* (to herald [the Sabbath]). Whatever its precise meaning, this has become known as the Trumpeting Stone.

The Royal Porch and the buildings immediately surrounding it were typically Roman in architectural style. The Royal Porch itself was a basilica that opened out on its north side into the open courtyard, which is often known as the Court of the Gentiles, but, as we have seen above, was in fact a Roman forum.

In his efforts to gain the Jewish people's favor, Herod attempted to bring the city of Jerusalem up to the architectural standard of other Roman cities, building this basilica and forum in a style similar to those in other cities of the Roman Empire.

The passages from the Double Gate and Triple Gate led under the Royal Porch and opened into this Outer Courtyard, just in front of the Hulda Gates leading into the original temple square. The north side of this Outer Courtyard adjoined the south side of the five-hundred-cubit square, where the temple proper began. Another passage led from a low-level street outside in the Tyropoeon Valley through Barclay's Gate into this Outer Courtyard. So a worshiper could enter from the west side of the temple through Barclay's Gate, or ascend the monumental staircase into the western end of the Royal Porch, or go through the Double or Triple Gates and up into this Outer Courtyard area.

From this Outer Courtyard, people entered the five-hundred-cubit square Temple Mount through the Hulda Gates on the south wall of the inner five-hundred-cubit square. People gathered together here in great numbers and could shelter in the porches on its east and west sides. Here too a huge trade went on, as the priests sold cattle and sheep, doves, wood, precious jewels, and everything else the people needed for their sacrifices.

7. The Inner Courts of the Temple

We come now to the innermost courtyard of the temple, the temple court. As the worshiper progressed inwards from the outer courts and porches to the original Temple Mount square and to the temple court, each area was considered holier than the previous one, as we have seen. The holiest place of all was, of course, the Holy of Holies within the temple sanctuary. The holier the court, the more stringently were temple rules and regulations enforced.

A terrace ran right around the outside of the temple court, though we have little written evidence about it. Twelve steps led up to this terrace, or raised platform, from which some of the gates led directly into the temple's inner courts. The Mishnah states that seven gates were positioned around the temple court, some entering from the top of the platform, some from the bottom directly from the Court of Israel; but it is unclear where these gates actually stood. My model shows nine gates, because it includes the Court of the Women at the east side of the temple court, added by Herod; whereas the Mishnah describes the temple court as it was before the Court of the Women was built, when there were indeed seven gates.

Some of the buildings constituting the temple court projected beyond the lines of the five-hundred-cubit square. Although most scholars suppose the terrace ran around the Temple Court in straight lines, it is possible that it ran in and out around the projecting buildings. The evidence about this terrace raises a

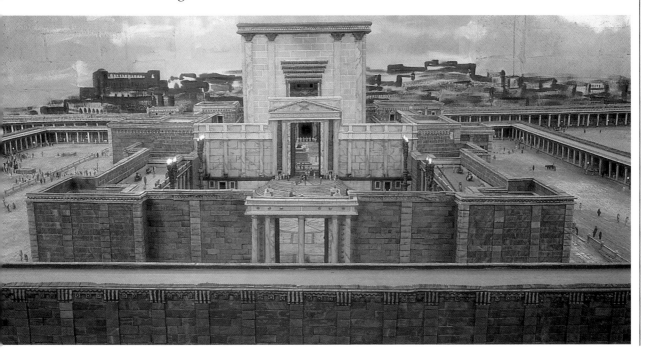

View of the temple from the east, showing the succession of courts, culminating in the Holy of Holies.

number of problems. We read in different sources of twelve steps up to the terrace; of fifteen steps up from the Court of the Women; and of twelve steps up from the Court of the Priests. Some scholars even claim that the Court of the Women was not surrounded by a platform at all. All these different flights of steps and levels have to be reconciled—not an easy matter!

Three gates on the south side of the temple court, each with a different function, led from the terrace into the Court of the Priests. The Wood Gate, at the west end, may have been entered from the building that extended outward, with the gate at the same level as the Court of Israel. The Water Gate may also have projected outward.

On the east side of the Temple Court, the Eastern Gate was approached by means of fifteen Steps of Ascent. On the north side of the temple court stood the Gate of the Flame, probably entered from the top of the terrace, as was the Sacrifice Gate, through which the sacrifices were brought in. According to the Mishnah, the gate that led into the Chamber of the Hearth seems to have been entered from the Court of Israel. After the Court of Prayer was added, making it one-third larger, the Court of Israel was almost twice the size of the inner temple court. On the south side of the Court of Israel there was just one gate, the Women's Gate; on the east side, the Gate of the Pure and the Just; and on the north side, the Music Gate.

Inner Porches

The inner porches, or colonnades, that surrounded the five-hundred-cubit square Temple Mount, were lower and smaller than the outer porches. The Mishnah and Josephus give us no details about them, so our knowledge is inadequate. However, the Mishnah describes the gates through which people entered this area, implying there was a boundary marker, probably in the form of a colonnade. Many scholars think this was the partition, known as the *soreg*, mentioned by Josephus. However, the Mishnah talks about coming from the Hulda Gates and *then* reaching the partition that separates the Court of the Gentiles from the Court of Israel.

A marble screen, known as the Wall of Partition, or *soreg* in Hebrew, separated the holy temple courts from the Court of the Gentiles. Inscriptions in Latin and Greek, set up at each of the openings in this wall, warned non-Jewish strangers not to proceed into the holy areas beyond, under penalty of death. A stone inscription to this effect was discovered in Jerusalem in 1871, engraved on a block of limestone 57 x 85 centimeters (22 x 33 inches). It reads: "No stranger is to enter within the balustrade around the temple and enclosure. Whoever is caught will be responsible for his own death, which will ensue." The New Testament also refers to this "Wall of Partition" in Acts 21:26ff and Ephesians 2:14–18, and it is described in *Middot* 2.1. It is not known whether this wall went all the way around the temple court, or, as some scholars believe, only along the south side.

Any Gentile who wished to be accepted into the Jewish faith had to become a proselyte. There were two kinds of proselyte: the "proselyte at the gate" could go no further than the *soreg* partition and had to watch the ceremonies from a distance. But the "proselyte of the Law", having undergone baptism and circumcision and met all the other requirements of the Jewish Law, could go through the partition. Having been accepted as a Jew, he could take part in the main temple ceremonies.

While the south, west, and north sides of the Temple Mount were surrounded by the colonnades described above, Solomon's Porch, on the east side of the Temple Mount, was much larger and more imposing. It formed part of the eastern wall but did not extend for its whole length. Beyond the south, west, and north sides of the earlier five-hun-

Bird's-eye view of the temple model, showing the inner Temple Court and the magnificent steps leading up to the Nicanor Gate.

red-cubit-square Temple Mount there were Herodian extensions, but none beyond Solomon's Porch, which, despite its name, did not in fact date from Solomon's time. Because this porch was in a much better state of repair than the rest of the buildings when Herod came to rebuild the temple (it had perhaps been renovated shortly before his time), he did not disturb it. Solomon's Porch stood partly in the Court of Israel and partly in the Court of the Gentiles; and here Rabbis sat and taught. Indeed, we read that Jesus and his disciples taught from Solomon's Porch, which was reserved mainly for teaching (John 10:23). Shields, tapestries, and trophies gained in battle, or presented to Israel by foreign kings, were hung all along the walls, making it a place of great solemnity.

Near the north end of Solomon's Porch was the Shushan Gate, through which (as described above) the scapegoat and the red heifer were led out across the Kidron Valley to the Mount of Olives.

8. The Inner Gates of the Temple

We have considered previously the temple area's external gates, and now discuss the gates within the original Temple Mount square. These gates served a variety of purposes, some being vital to the every-day running of the temple, others little used. There were five gates into the inner courts. The Eastern Gate to the Temple Mount served as the exterior Eastern Gate as well. It was also known as the Shushan Gate, as we have seen. In addition, there were two gates on the south side of the temple court, known as the Hulda Gates; one on the west, the Coponius Gate; and one on the north, the Tadi Gate.

Within the temple court were yet more

The great doors of the Eastern, or Nicanor, Gate here shown closed. The priests could also use the little doors on each side of the gates.

gates: another eastern gate, the Gate of the Pure and Just; four gates on the south side, the Women's Gate, the Water Gate, the Gate of the Firstborn, and the Wood Gate; and another four on the north side, the Gate of the Music, the Gate of the Flame, the Sacrifice Gate, and the Beth-Moked Gate. The Nicanor Gate, in the center of the temple court, divided the Court of the Women from the Court of the Priests. Finally, there was the entrance gate to the sanctuary itself. There were, of course, many smaller gates into rooms in addition to the major entrances.

The gates in the temple not only were openings in a wall but they also formed buildings in their own right, containing rooms where various activities were carried out. Each gate had two or three stories and was manned by officials and guards. While some gates were open for anyone to enter, others were restricted to select groups of people. Everything was strictly controlled, and anyone suspicious was quickly turned away.

The Mishnah refers to three eastern gates, without distinguishing between them. I believe the principal eastern gate was the Nicanor Gate, sometimes known as the Gate of Corinthian Brass, standing between the Court of the Priests and the Court of Prayer. The Nicanor Gate was named after an Alexandrian who donated this splendid gate, crafted from Corinthian bronze, to the temple. The Mishnah describes many ceremonies that took place in and around this gate.

The Mishnah also refers to another eastern gate, outside the Nicanor Gate

Left: **From the Nicanor Gate the priests could see across the Court of the Women and up to the Mount of Olives.**

vith which it is often confused, the Gate of the Palace of Shushan, or Shushan Gate, which looked out directly over the Kidron Valley to the Mount of Olives. This gate has been described previously.

A third eastern gate, known as the Gate of the Pure and Just, led into the Court of Prayer and was the main entrance used by dignitaries.

Gates into the Temple Mount

The Hulda Gates, or General Entrance Gates, were situated on the south side of the five-hundred-cubit-square Temple Mount. The name Hulda is usually understood to have been derived from the prophetess of the same name (2 Kings 2:14; 2 Chronicles 34:22). There were two sets of Hulda Gates: the eastern set of gates for the priests and the other set for the laypeople. These gates were entered from the Outer Courtyard, though priests reporting for duty usually entered through the Triple Gate in the southern wall of the temple complex, passing through the underground passageway, and up the stairs just in front of the priestly Hulda Gates, then enter-

ing the Court of the Gentiles through these gates. It is unclear from the Mishnah where the priests went after this. Although this gate separated the priests from the rest of the worshipers, it is difficult to see how they could remain apart, because they then had to proceed to their living quarters to collect their priestly garments. Perhaps they then went through the Gate of the Wood or the Gate of the Flame.

Any worshiper, Jew or Gentile, could pass through the non-priestly Hulda Gates into the Court of the Gentiles. This route led through the southern external wall of the temple, then through a passage west of the passage from the Triple Gate, and up a staircase to arrive at the Hulda Gates. I believe it was through these gates, rather than through the Shushan, or Eastern, Gate that Jesus made his triumphant entry on Palm Sunday (Matthew 21:12). The Court of the Gentiles had a small porch where various activities went on, including money-changing to enable people to pay their temple tribute in the correct coinage.

We have very little information about the Coponius Gate, on the west side of the Temple Mount, except that it was named after a Roman general who contributed to its construction. This gate opened onto the Outer Courtyard, from which a bridge, supported by Wilson's Arch, led to the wealthy, upper city, where the high priests and Herod himself had their palaces. Through this gate, the wealthy, high-ranking, and distinguished entered, keeping apart from the ordinary people. Like the Hulda Gates, the Coponius Gate was much smaller than the gates surrounding the temple court.

On the north side of the Temple Mount was located the Tadi Gate, which the Mishnah states was never used. It is unclear what period this refers to, but it is quite obvious that it must have been used, especially in the time of Herod and Jesus when huge numbers of people vis-

The Gate of the Pure and Just is the eastern gate leading into the Court of the Women.

ited the temple. The Tadi Gate was similar to the Hulda and Coponius Gates and led from the northern Outer Courtyard where so much went on. Animals were brought in from the outer Northern Gate and kept here for people to collect when they were needed for sacrifice. Possibly worshipers themselves also entered by this gate.

The original Tadi Gate, dating from the time of Solomon's Temple, was built at a lower level, since this northern Outer Courtyard was originally the Beza Valley, filled in by Pompey's soldiers in 63 B.C., to enable them to storm the temple. Remains of the original Tadi Gate have been discovered at the end of the tunnel that runs beneath Chamber 1, according to Warren's numbering. When Herod rebuilt the temple, the Tadi Gate was reconstructed at a higher level. "Tadi Gate" is Hebrew for Gate of the Lambs, and it was through this gate that lambs and other sacrifices, including the red heifer and the scapegoat, were brought in. They were then taken through the Sacrifice Gate in the inner temple court and into the Court of the Priests.

The Court of Prayer, also called the Court of the Women, formed the eastern part of the temple court. There was originally no separate court here, and in Solomon's time the temple court was open to the Eastern Gate, with chambers built around it later to house materials needed for running the temple. This tended to restrict the movement of the crowds gathered around the Nicanor Gate during the main festivals. In Herod's Temple there were gates on all four sides of the Court of Prayer, including the Nicanor Gate on the west, which led into the Court of the Men and Court of the Priests.

Two small doors on each side of the Nicanor Gate gave access to the chambers containing the musical instruments that the Levites played on the platform in front of the Nicanor Gate. The Levites also recited the fifteen Psalms of Ascent (Psalms 120–134), standing on the fifteen semicircular steps between the Court of the Women and the Court of the Israelites.

The main entrance into the Court of Prayer was a gate on the south side known as the General Entrance Gate or Women's Gate. Three steps led up from the Court of Israel to this large and magnificent gate. Like the other gates was elaborately decorated with gold and silver and ornamented all around the outside. It was to this temple gate that the apostles Peter and John went to pray (Acts 3:2). This area was intended for the use of the general public who came into the temple.

Outside each of the gates that led into the temple court were places for people to wash their feet. Everyone had to wash in the sacred baths before entering the temple court, but after leaving the baths, they could possibly become defiled again by walking in the steps of someone who was unclean. As a precaution, worshipers usually washed their feet a second time before entering the temple court.

East of, and immediately opposite, the Nicanor Gate stood the Gate of the Pure and the Just, another important eastern gate, often mistakenly called the Beautiful Gate. It was unlawful for anyone ritually unclean, such as a lame man, to enter this gate or even to sit outside it. This special gate was more elaborately decorated than those on the south or north sides, since it was used by those who considered themselves highly favored in God's sight—the wealthy, the important, and those with responsible positions. They would enjoy the praise and honor of onlookers as they entered into the courtyard through this gate to make extravagant offerings.

According to the Mishnah, when the red heifer was sacrificed, its ashes were put in jars. One jar was left on the Mount of Olives to be used when another red heifer was sacrificed, after the ashes from the previous red heifer had been completely consumed. A second jar was placed in the temple for the priests to use for purification and cleansing. A third jar of ashes was placed on the terrace surrounding the Court of the Women, just outside the Gate of the Pure and the Just, indicating that there must have been some sort of raised platform around this part of the temple.

The Gate of Music stands north of, and

exactly opposite, the General Entrance Gate, to which it was almost identical. The temple's music and singing were renowned throughout the ancient world, and it was here that the temple musicians sometimes stood. Processions often came from the Eastern, or Nicanor, Gate, down the steps and across the courtyard, out of the Gate of Music, around and back in again; hence the name, the Gate of Music.

Across the Court of the Priests from the sanctuary stood the gate known in Herod's day as the Nicanor Gate. This gate was about nine meters (thirty feet) wide and eighteen meters (sixty feet) high, constructed of bronze and extremely heavy, making it very difficult to open and close. It was even bigger than the gate

Top: **The Beth-Moked Gate, the main entrance to the Chamber of the Hearth, which housed the priests.**

Bottom: **Priests enter the Hulda Gate.**

A view of the traders' stalls outside the Hulda Gate

The Gate of the Music, where the temple musicians sometimes stood at festivals.

that led into the sanctuary itself. Before Herod extended the temple, this was known as the Eastern Gate. As we have seen, the temple was built to the same basic plan as the tabernacle, and it was to this Eastern Gate that people brought their sacrifices and presented them to the priests in both places of worship.

The Nicanor Gate stood between the Court of Prayer (the Court of the Women) and the Court of the Men and the Court of the Priests, and only priests and men who were ritually clean according to the temple laws could enter it. Immediately inside this gate was the Court of the Men, and, farther inside, the Court of the Priests.

Every day at sundown, when the services and ceremonies had finished, the Nicanor Gate was locked, not to be reopened until the next morning. The gates around this area—the entrance to the sanctuary, the southern and northern gates and this eastern Nicanor Gate—represented the curtains of the original tabernacle and were all locked at night. This entire sacred area, which included the temple sanctuary itself, the Court of the Priests, the Court of the Men, the surrounding buildings, and the Nicanor Gate, represented the tabernacle in which the Israelites worshiped during their desert wanderings.

Early in the morning, when the priests were preparing for the day's services and sacrifices, a priest stood on the Place of Trumpeting, watching for dawn, which would be heralded by the outline of the Hebron mountains becoming visible. On cloudy days, it was difficult to decide when the sun was rising, but as soon as the priest saw the outline of the Hebron mountains, he gave the signal for the huge doors of the Nicanor Gate to be opened. Then the side doors and the doors to the sanctuary were opened, after which the lamb was offered for the morning sacrifice.

The Mishnah states that it took twenty men to open just one of the mighty doors of the Nicanor Gate, so one can imagine how heavy they were. This great gate was flanked by two small side gates, which worshipers could use if they wished. Once the gates were open, the people brought their sacrifices to the priests to be inspected, and accepted or rejected. The priests stood at the Nicanor Gate to lead the services and ceremonies and to address the people gathered in the Court of Prayer (or Court of the Women).

On the west side of the Court of the Priests there were no official temple gates, only two smaller gates used to bring in supplies and take away refuse.

The most easterly gate on the north side of the Temple Mount was the Gate of the Flame, or Gate of the Spark, named after the light that burned continually above it. If any other light or fire within the temple was extinguished, it could be rekindled from this flame. The Gate of the Flame was almost exactly opposite another gate, on the south side of this courtyard, of about the same size, shape, and appearance. A general entrance for those qualified to pass through it, this was much smaller than the Nicanor Gate but also opened out on to the terrace that led up and into the Court of the Men.

The Gate of the Flame had chambers on each side of it. One of them was called the Chamber of the Shekel, where the temple tribute was paid. People who earlier had exchanged their money near the Hulda Gates brought their temple tax to the priest here.

Further west was the Sacrifice Gate, where all public sacrifices were taken into the temple. Like the Gate of the Flame, it led from the terrace into the Court of the Priests and Court of the Men. On both sides of this gateway stood chambers where it is said that at least six animals were constantly kept ready for sacrifice. The original tabernacle had only an eastern gate, where all sacrifices were taken in and out. However, in the

temple, sacrificial animals were taken in through the north-facing Sacrifice Gate and offered as required. If they had to be taken out afterward, as were the red heifer and the scapegoat, the route was through the Nicanor Gate.

The animals for sacrifice were collected together in pens on the north side of the temple, near the Northern Gate, on the outer edge of the temple complex. Here the animals were received, washed, and made ready for offering.

A small side gate provided entry when all other gates were locked and barred. This gate was left unlocked for people to go in and out after the main gates had been bolted inside. One priest was in charge of the key. It is said that after he locked the gates, he put the key under a slab in the Chamber of the Hearth, where the priests lived while on duty, and slept

The great gates leading into the temple sanctuary, with four columns decorated with a golden vine. Only priests could enter these gates.

on it, so that nobody could get the key without disturbing him.

There were three gates to the Chamber of the Hearth, two on the north side. Next came the Beth-Moked Gate, the main entrance to the Chamber of the Hearth, and where priestly officials and ordinary priests were located. The priest in charge of receipts sat here, so if a worshiper wished to buy a lamb or bull, he paid for it here, then went to collect the animal he wanted. Often people tried to get an animal without paying for it, so the priests checked to see if they were telling the truth. If somebody said he had lost his receipt, the receipts were added up at the end of the day to see if they tallied with the animals sold. This again was an entrance only for priests who lived, slept, and ate here while on duty.

The Chamber of the Hearth had three stories. The north-facing gate, where the receipts were issued, was situated on the ground floor. The side gate was a little higher, on the terrace that led into the temple courts. Another gate, on the opposite side of this building, led from the first floor where the priests were accommodated, into the Court of the Priests where they went to serve.

On the south side of the Court of the Priests were three more gates vital to running the temple. Twelve steps led up from the Court of Israel to the Water Gate, the most easterly of these gates, which was elaborately decorated like every other major gate. The Water Gate led into the Court of the Men and was surrounded by buildings used for the administration of the temple. It was called the Water Gate because on the Feast of Tabernacles the high priest progressed from there to the Pool of Siloam, took up a golden vessel of water, and brought it back. The other priests accompanied him, blowing trumpets, and the people followed in procession, across the temple site and in through the Water Gate, waving palm and willow branches and carrying fruit. Although women had to stay outside the gate, the men could proceed as far as the Court of the Men, while the priests went into the Court of the Priests, circling the altar and sprinkling water around it.

A similar procession took place early every morning during this seven-day feast, immediately after the priest gave the signal from the Place of Trumpeting and just as the morning sacrifice was being offered. While the Water Gate had this special function at the Feast of Tabernacles, it served at other times as a general entrance, and any qualified person could pass through it.

The central gate on this south side of the Court of the Priests was the Gate of the Firstborn. All three gates on this side were similar in size and shape, differing just a little in decoration. The Gate of the Firstborn, too, was entered from the Court of Israel, but was reserved solely for the use of Jewish people coming to pay their redemption money. Every first born child or animal was, according to the Law of Moses, God's property, and redemption money had to be paid to meet the requirements of this law. There has been much speculation as to how much the redemption money, which, in effect, amounted to a tax, amounted to. It is difficult to calculate, but we know it was substantial and only the relatively well-off would come and pay the priests at this gate.

The most westerly of these gates on the south side of the Court of the Priests was the Wood Gate, which was similar in appearance to the other two. Worshipers who wanted to make an offering of wood came to this gate. It is often imagined that Jewish sacrifices were restricted to lambs, bulls, and doves; but a variety of other offerings was acceptable, including wood. All these items were offered for sale by the priests on the temple site. Offerings of wood were brought to this gate for inspection by the priests. Only wood of a specified type and quality was accepted. If there was any infection or decay, or if it was the wrong wood, it was rejected.

The Women's Gate.

The gates leading into the temple sanctuary itself were enormous, some twenty cubits high and ten cubits wide, and they were constructed in such a way that they folded back double against the wall. There were two sets of sanctuary gates. The outer set, folding outward, was separated by a gap the thickness of the wall from the inner set, which opened inward and folded back against the interior wall. These sanctuary gates were magnificently decorated with gold and silver, and only the priests were allowed to enter the Holy Place through them.

The massive sanctuary gates were designed so that they could be locked from the inside. On each side of the main sanctuary gates was a smaller gate, of which the more southerly gate was always kept shut; it is written in Ezekiel 44:2 that when God entered into the temple, he shut the door and it was never to be opened. The priests entered through the more northerly door to open the main doors. Through a passage in the wall, they could obtain access to the space between the two sets of doors to open them. Both sets of doors then folded back against the walls. A great blue curtain hung just inside these sanctuary doors, to prevent the laypeople in the courtyards outside from seeing into the sanctuary.

The sanctuary gates were supported on four columns, each decorated with a golden vine wreathed around it. The Mishnah (*Middot* 3.8) records that "Whoever gave a leaf, a berry or a cluster as a freewill offering, brought it and the priests hung it there." Josephus agrees with the Mishnah and adds that the sanctuary doors were "a marvel of size and artistry to all who saw with what costliness of material it had been constructed" (*Antiquities* 15.395). Jesus possibly had in mind these golden vines in front of the sanctuary doors when he said, "I am the true vine and my Father is the husbandman" (John 15:1). Two vents above the sanctuary gates allowed the incense burning on the altar of incense to pervade the temple.

9. The Court of the Priests

Steps led down from the front of the temple sanctuary into the Court of the Priests. Near the foot of these steps stood a device with ten mechanically-blown pipes. This was not a musical instrument, but a means of signaling instructions to the priests carrying out the ceremonies. It is claimed that, when sounded, these pipes could be heard as far as Jericho—some ten miles away.

Just south of these pipes stood the laver, the huge bronze container holding the water that the priests used while serving in the temple. It is believed that any water remaining in the laver at the end of the day was emptied out and used to wash down the Court of the Priests, where so much slaughter of sacrificed animals took place.

We know that the bronze laver in Solomon's Temple rested upon twelve bronze oxen. Although the nineteenth-century writer Alfred Edersheim claimed that the laver in Herod's Temple rested upon twelve bronze lions, I cannot find evidence to support this. It is unclear whether it rested upon lions or oxen. When the priests came to wash, they drew water from the laver by means of a tap fitted to a lion's (or ox's) mouth.

In the Temple Court, there were thirteen veils and thirteen tables. One of the latter was the table of showbread (Leviticus 24:1–9). Of the other two tables situated in the Holy Porch, one was of marble, the other of gold. Two more tables stood west of the altar, one of marble, one of silver; while eight more tables were located near the Shambles, the place where the sacrificial animals were slaughtered, dissected, and prepared for people to eat or for burning. The Shambles were situated on the north side of the Court of the Priests, which was also north of the altar, and, according to the Mishnah, the most sacred side. Here the holiest creatures were slaughtered and offered as sacrifices.

The altar of burnt offerings itself stood in front of the temple and was a tall, stone structure upon which the priests offered the sacrifices. Normally, two separate fires were kept burning on the altar, but on special occasions, such as the Day of Atonement, four fires burned, one on each of its corners.

According to *Middot*, the altar measured thirty-two cubits square and was approached from the west by a ramp, up which the priests walked, carrying animals, blood, and other items necessary for performing sacrifices. Josephus describes it as thirty cubits square and fifteen cubits high (*War* 5.225). There was a horn on each corner of the altar, with a channel cut into each horn down which blood, water, and oil was poured. A red line ran around the altar half-way up to act as a guide for priests during the sacrifices. Sometimes sacrificial blood had to be dashed against the altar below this line, sometimes sprinkled above it.

The altar was a highly symbolic structure, standing immediately in front of the temple. Much blood was sprinkled, dashed, or thrown against the altar, and this, together with the fires that burned on it continually, presented a major cleansing problem. Every Sabbath, when the temple was comparatively quiet, the

priests cleaned the altar. In addition, twice a year the entire altar was freshly white-washed.

The Buildings Around the Court of the Priests

The buildings and chambers around the Court of the Priests played a vital part in the life of the temple. Most of the information we possess about these buildings derives from the Mishnah, though some is found in the Old Testament, notably in the description of the building of Solomon's Temple (1 Kings 6). There is very little information available from archaeological sources.*

On the east side of the Court of the Priests stood the Nicanor, or Eastern, Gate, the main entrance for worshipers from the Court of the Women. From the Nicanor Gate, a colonnade with buildings incorporated into it ran around the east, south, and north sides of the Court of the Priests. On the east side of the Court of the Priests, both north and south of the Nicanor Gate, stood the Hall of the Priests, occupying half the colonnade on each side of the gate. Then came the Hall of the Levites, elevated by two large steps.

In the southeast corner of the Court of the Priests stood the Hall of Polished Stones, in Hebrew, *gazith*; a large and important building where the Sanhedrin sat as the supreme court, before the Royal Porch and other Herodian extensions were added. After these additions, as we have seen, the Sanhedrin sat at the east end of the Royal Porch. The original Sanhedrin Court would have decided matters concerning the law of the land, secular rather than solely religious matters. But in Herod's time, the Hall of Polished Stones was used solely to decide Jewish religious matters, which were of no concern to the Roman occupying power. In this building all major decisions about the priesthood and the running of the temple were made. If alterations, extensions, or other building work were needed in the temple area, the Sanhedrin had to convene here, in the Hall of Polished Stones, to decide what was to be done. In Herod's day, the Sanhedrin sitting in the Royal Porch, although presided over by Jewish judges, was controlled by the Roman authorities.

The place of slaughter, north of the altar, where animals were prepared for sacrifice.

Next page: **Bird's-eye view of the Court of the Priests and altar of burnt offerings.**

* *The Messiah of the Temple According to the Tractate Middot*, by Joseph Patrich, illustrated by Leen Ritmeyer, based upon information from the Mishnah, is particularly helpful.

View of the Court of the Priests, showing the great altar of sacrifice, and in the foreground the tethering place for animals intended for sacrifice.

Peter and John were brought to the Hall of Polished Stones to be arraigned before the Sanhedrin (Acts 4:5–22). But when Jesus was taken for trial to the Sanhedrin, this court was sitting in the Royal Porch, thereby admitting Roman jurisdiction (Matthew 26:57–68).

South of the Hall of Polished Stones was the Pancake Maker's Chamber, which is described in the Mishnah. The priests met in this corner early each morning to eat a sacramental meal, after having left their quarters in the Chamber of the Hearth and circled the temple, one group to the south and the other to the north. After this breakfast, they cast lots to decide who was to serve in which capacity at the morning sacrifice.

In the northeast corner of the Court of the Priests stood the Parwah Chamber, which incorporated other rooms including the Vestment Keeper's Office, where the priests picked up their special garments as they came on duty. Having collected these priestly garments, they then went to the underground sacred bath, where they washed to purify themselves in preparation. Then, dressed in their uniforms, the priests took their every-

day clothes back to the Hall of the Priest and left them in one of ninety-six lock ers fitted along its east wall. Their clothes remained here until the priests had com pleted their term of duty in the temple.

On the lower level of the Parwah Chamber were situated the Chamber o Rinsing, or Chamber of Washing, and the Chamber of Salt. A huge sewer ran through these chambers and under the building, fed by drains from the altar and from the place of slaughter, and eventu ally emptied into the Kidron Valley. This sewer, described in the Mishnah, has never actually been discovered; but believe it was located here. The priest had to take care to keep this sewer clean as it could easily become blocked by all the refuse washed down into it from the area of sacrifices above.

Nearby, on top of the porch where a balcony ran around, was a sacred bath where the high priest washed on the Day of Atonement. On this day he had to strip and completely immerse himself, chang ing his clothes five times and washing his hands and feet ten times.

Adjoining the Parwah Chamber wa the Gate of the Flame, or Gate of Kindling (or Spark), so called because a flame was kept burning over it continuously. Guards kept watch above this gate. It was immediately opposite the Water Gate, on the other side of the court, which was similarly guarded. Further chambers were incorporated into this gate.

Also close to the Parwah Chamber, but outside the temple court, was the Chamber of the Curtain. The Mishnah (*Shekalim* 8.5) tells us that here eighty-two young women continuously wove veils and curtains for the temple. (If this chamber had been located inside the temple court, it would have been too "holy" for women to come and work here.)

Adjoining the Gate of the Flame were other chambers, including the Chamber of the Skins, where the skins of sacrificed animals were taken to be offered for sale by the priests. Anyone making an offering of wine or oil had to present it in the skin of an animal that had been sacrificed in the temple, so they had to buy a suitable skin here. Next to the Chamber of the Skins was the Chamber of the Lambs.

Close to this, possibly on the east side of the Gate of the Flame, was the Chamber of the Shekel, where the temple tribute was paid. Just before Passover, men over the age of twenty came to the Gate of the Flame to pay their temple tribute. After the temple was extended within the Court of Prayer (or Court of the Women), collecting boxes were set up there for people to pay their tribute money. However, before the Court of the Women was added, tribute money was paid in the Chamber of the Shekel.

All these buildings were closely connected, with a balcony linking their upper floors and a passage at basement level giving access to all of them—the Chamber of the Lambs and the Chamber of the Sacrifices as well as a side door running off the terrace through which the priests could enter or leave when all the main gates were locked.

South of the Parwah Chamber and along the south side of the Court of the Priests, was the Water, or *Golah*, Room, where the water supply was controlled. A waterwheel standing directly over

An underground room in the priests' Chamber of the Hearth.

This great basin, or laver, stood in the Court of the Priests and was drained and filled daily.

Chamber 5 (by Warren's numbering)—a rock-hewn passage that led into the temple water cisterns—drew water from the chambers beneath to fill the laver. The plumbing system was designed, so the Mishnah tells us (*Yom* 3.10), by Ben Katin, who also designed the laver itself and the system for filling it with water.

According to Jewish law, if water intended for religious purposes was conveyed from one place to another in a bucket or other vessel, it was no longer *kosher*. Therefore, water for the temple had to be collected as rainwater, as surface water, or from a stream, and never carried into the temple. So water was drawn up from underground by this wheel and the laver filled from it every morning. The laver was emptied every evening, to keep it fit for sacred use.

Next to the Water Room was the Chamber of the Captives. All these buildings were linked by interconnecting gates.

The Chamber of the Hearth, or Beth-Moked Chamber, at the northwest corner, was where the priests lived while on duty. This building had a lower basement, basement, ground floor, and top floor. The priests slept in the central, first-floor chamber and ate in the ground floor, which was large, with various apartments. In one corner of this central chamber, the showbread was baked. In another corner, lambs were prepared for the priests' use at Passover. A staircase

Chambers Above Ground (page 61)

1. Holy of Holies
2. Holy Place
3. Temple Porch
4. Chambers of the Utensils
5. Side Chambers
6. Stairway to Roof
7. Chamber of the Curtain
8. Chamber of the Lambs
9. Chamber of Skins; Chamber of Salt below
10. Chamber of the Hearth
11. Parwah Chamber; Rinsing Chamber and Guard room below
12. Vestment Keeper's Office
13. Pancake-maker's Chamber
14. Chamber of Stone; Chamber of Wood below; Chamber of High Priests above
15. Chamber of Captives
16. Golah Chamber
17. Chamber of Hewn Stone (Gazith)
18. Hall of Israelites
19. Hall of Priests
20. Chamber of Lepers
21. Chamber of the Wood
22. Chamber of Oils and Wines
23. Chamber of Nazirites
24. The Treasury; Chamber of Musical Instruments below
25. Immersion pools
26. Administration buildings

Temple Chambers above ground

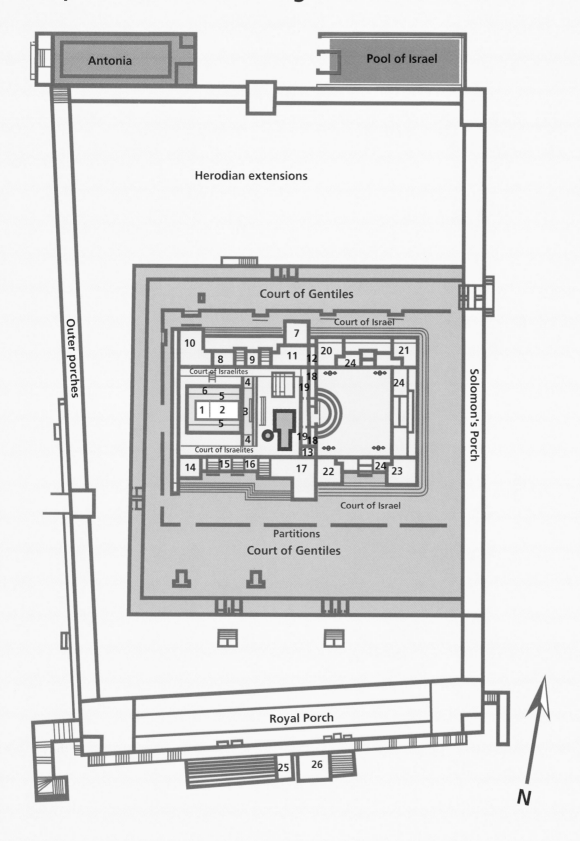

Antonia

Pool of Israel

Herodian extensions

Outer porches

Court of Gentiles

Court of Israel

10

7

8　9

11　12　20

21

24

Court of Israelites

4

18

19

6

5

24

1　2　3

5

4

19　18

13

Solomon's Porch

14　15　16

17

22　24　23

Court of Israelites

Court of Israel

Partitions
Court of Gentiles

Royal Porch

25　26

N

in a third corner led down to underground Chamber 3, which housed the sacred baths in which the priests washed and purified themselves.

Above this were the priests' sleeping quarters, furnished with stone benches around the walls, on which, according to the Mishnah, the elderly priests could sleep, while the younger priests slept on the floor. Set into the floor was a compartment where the temple keys were concealed overnight after all the doors had been locked. The priest in charge of the gates placed the keys here and slept over the compartment to keep them secure.

Above the priests' dormitory was a store chamber for the utensils and materials needed to run the Chamber of the Hearth. From the central floor, a gate led into the Court of the Priests, from which the priests went out early in the morning to start their day's service, as described above.

At the southwest corner of the Court of the Priests stood the House of Stone, or Chamber of the Honorable Councillors, where the priests gathered to make everyday decisions about running the temple. In this chamber, scribes copied the Scriptures continuously, along with documents needed to administer the temple. At the top of the House of Stone were rooms where the high priest resided when he wanted to stay in the temple.

On special occasions, such as the Day of Atonement, the high priest had to spend a whole week in this apartment, preparing himself for the complex ceremonies, which had to be performed exactly right. The readings, recitals, benedictions, and sacrifices all had to be carried out in set order, and the high priest himself had to remain apart from everyone else so that he was ritually pure and clean, ready to perform his duties. If he were to become ritually unclean, he would be disqualified from completing his duties.

There was a sacred bath in the House of Stone where the high priest could wash at any time. The high priest's deputy remained with him during these rituals, and prepared himself too, in case the high priest, because of illness or disqualification through ritual uncleanness, was unable to carry out his solemn duties on the Day of Atonement.

There were no buildings on the west side of the Court of the Priests, as the temple itself stood close to its west boundary. But outside the Court, and on a lower level, stood two entrances, on the north and south sides, leading into underground chambers and passages through which the priests could enter any of the buildings. There was also an underground passage leading out into the Court of the Priests and another down into the sacred washing area.

10. The Court of Prayer

At the east end of the Court of the Priests was the Court of Prayer, more often called the Court of the Women, because this marked the limit beyond which women could not go. As we have seen, the Court of Prayer was a later addition to the temple court, and we are unsure whether the terrace went all around it, and if so, at what level. Like many scholars, I believe there were some steps and a raised platform. The Court of Prayer occupied approximately one third of the temple court area.

According to the Mishnah (*Middot* .–5), the walls of the Court of Prayer were erected first, followed by a balcony, forming porches all the way around, with a chamber forty cubits square at each corner. Many writers believe that these corner chambers extended into the court, but this could not have been so, as this would so greatly have reduced the size of the Court of Prayer that it could not have fulfilled its purpose as a gathering-place. I believe these four corner chambers ran out and over the terrace that ran around the outside of the Court of Prayer, and that the porch and terrace were together about forty cubits wide.

The four corner chambers each had different names and served various purposes: the Wood Chamber was in the northeast corner; the Chamber of the Leper in the northwest corner; the Nazirite Chamber in the southeast corner; and the Chamber of Oil and Wine in the southwest corner.

The Court of the Women, so called not because it was exclusively for women, but because this was the furthest that women could go into the temple precincts. Notice the assistant carrying oil up to the great lampstand (*left*).

The Chamber of Oil and Wine, showing the careful storage of these important commodities.

The Wood Chamber, in the northeast corner of the Court of Prayer, was a storeplace for the wood presented to, and accepted by, the temple. This timber was sorted and graded according to its intended purpose. It is said that when a priest was found guilty of some offense, he was dressed in black and sent to the Wood Chamber to sort wood, separating out rotten wood, timber infested with insects, and wood that was ritually unclean.

In the northwest corner of the Court of Prayer stood the Chamber of the Leper, which has mystified many writers since those with leprosy were not allowed into the temple area. However, this chamber was intended for use in the readmission into society of those who had been cleansed from the disease. If a man recovered from leprosy, the Jewish law stipulated that he had to show himself to a priest, not just outside the temple, but outside the city. In fact, the man had to be inspected closely by two priests.

If pronounced clean, the man cured from leprosy had to undergo a very elaborate ceremony in the wilderness involving two birds (Leviticus 14:1–9). After this, he was still not allowed into the city or into the temple for another seven days when he had to return to the priests for a further inspection. If then found to be clean, he was allowed into the Chamber of the Leper in the temple, where he underwent another elaborate and humiliating ceremony (Leviticus 14:10–20) involving stripping and washing in sacred baths, and then being shaved and inspected yet again.

After a former sufferer from leprosy was found to be completely cleansed, he went to the Nicanor Gate, at the top of the fifteen Steps of Ascent, on the west side of the Court of Prayer, to complete his ceremonial cleansing, before he could enter the Court of the Men. First he had to put his big toe through the entrance, then his thumb, and finally his head and ears. His head was then anointed with il, and he was at last declared clean and allowed to proceed into the Court of the Men, or Court of Israel, beyond the Nicanor Gate.

Between the Chamber of the Leper and the Chamber of the Wood was the Gate of the Music, facing to the north of the Court of Prayer. During certain ceremonies, the temple musicians descended the fifteen Steps of Ascent and left by this gate, circulating and then reentering before climbing the steps again, all the time singing and playing.

In chambers beneath the southwest and northwest corners of the Court of the Women, and running under the Court of the Priests and its gates, were store places for the musical instruments the priests and Levites played in the temple during such ceremonies.

On the south side of the Court of Prayer stood the Chamber of Oil and Wine, where oil and wine for use in the temple ceremonies was stored. A large store place was necessary to contain the huge quantities of oil and wine consumed in the temple.

The Nazirite Chamber, in the southeast corner of the Court of Prayer, was set aside for people taking Nazirite vows.

It was considered very honorable, particularly for the wealthy, to come and make such a vow, which involved bringing a ram for sacrifice to the priest at the Nicanor Gate. The ram was slaughtered in the ordained manner, its blood dashed against the altar, and its unclean parts removed and burnt. The remainder of the ram's carcass was then taken to the Nazirite Chamber and boiled.

The Mishnah says the Nazirite's ram's meat was to be "sodden." It took me some time to realize that this meant that the flesh of the sacrificial animal was to be boiled, not roasted. A person taking the Nazirite vow also had to bring a basket of twelve loaves of unleavened bread, wafers, oil, and wine. When the ram had been cooked, the appropriate parts of the animal, together with the correct bread and wine, had to be handed over to the

priests. The Nazirite then ate the remainder himself.

A Nazirite vow also involved cutting the hair of the man taking the vow and throwing it under the pot in which the meat was boiled. Such a vow could take the form of a pledge to do something, an offering, or some sort of contribution—anything that could be vowed to the temple, the priests, or to other people. The shortest duration of a Nazirite vow was

Top: **The Chamber of the Leper, for receiving those who had been cleansed of this disease.**

Bottom: **The Wood Chamber, where timber was sorted, graded, and stored.**

thirty days, but it could extend almost indefinitely. Some men were lifelong Nazirites, although for most it involved just a short period of dedication.

A man taking a Nazirite vow was expected to put a freewill offering into the appropriate collection box in the temple, in addition to the offerings detailed above. If he broke the Nazirite vow, there was a severe penalty to pay, related to what he had offered. This could entail punishment with stripes, fines, or being forced to undergo further rituals.

Between the Wood Chamber and the Nazirite Chamber, on the east side of the Court of Prayer, stood the Gate of the Pure and the Just; a larger, more elaborate gate than those on the south and north sides of the court. The wealthy entered here and drew attention to themselves by placing generous—and noisy—contributions in the collecting boxes, as well as by making generous offerings to the priests in front of the Nicanor Gate. The general entrance gate, sometimes called the Women's Gate, was on the south side of the Court of Prayer and was for the use of ordinary people. People visiting the temple had to be wealthy, or at least quite well-off, to be able to meet all the requirements for sacrifices and offerings. Many people struggled to fulfil them, and if they could not meet their obligations, they felt shame before men and God.

The Four Lamps

Within the Court of Prayer stood four giant lamps, one in each corner. We read about them in the Mishnah (*Sukkot* 5.2–3) and elsewhere, but it is difficult to be sure exactly where they were located. Each lamp stood fifty cubits (twenty-six meters or eighty-five feet) high and was made of bronze, topped by five bowls each holding four lamps that were lit on special occasions. The Mishnah says that four young priests climbed ladders to light the lamps. Priests' cast-off garments were used to make wicks for these lamps, a fact that gives us some idea of their enormous size.

Many people who see my model confuse these four great lamps with the seven-branched golden lampstand that was located *inside* the temple sanctuary. The four lamps were enormous and consumed large quantities of oil when lit on three special festivals each year: Passover, Pentecost, and Tabernacles. The lamps were lit at Passover from sundown to midnight; at Pentecost from midnight to sunrise; and at Tabernacles from sundown to midnight. While the lamps remained alight, people could see them from a distance and celebrated with singing and dancing throughout the night. At the Feast of Tabernacles musicians were allowed to stand on the semicircular platform and entertain the people as they rejoiced before God.

A colonnade ran all around the outside of the Court of Prayer, with seats and places for people to meet. Senior rabbis met here, sitting together to teach and discuss.

The area within the Court of Prayer was also known as the treasury, because offerings were collected there. (The temple's actual wealth, however, was stored in thirty-eight chambers around the temple sanctuary, and was very secure.) Thirteen collecting boxes were set up all the way around the treasury; in my model, I have placed them in the recesses around the porches. These collecting boxes were called trumpets (*shofarot*) from the shape of their opening. An upturned trumpet-like opening with a large mouth led into a secure chest that stored the money. The mouth narrowed sharply to prevent people from putting their hands in to take money out.

Each collecting box was marked to indicate how the money dropped into it was to be used. Seven boxes were designated for compulsory offerings—temple dues and demands imposed on the people by the priests and by the religious laws. The other six boxes were designated for voluntary offerings: the first wo for the temple tribute, or temple shekel. We have mentioned above the Chamber of the Shekel, where the temple tribute was paid. Before the Court of Prayer was built, tribute was paid in the Court of the Priests; but afterwards, collecting boxes were placed here to receive the temple tribute (Mark 12:41–42).

Two other collecting boxes were for women to put money in to pay for the compulsory offerings of doves for their purification after childbirth. They did not buy the doves themselves but, after ascertaining the price from the officer in charge of the doves, they put the correct amount in the appropriate collecting box. At the end of the day, just before the evening sacrifice, the money was taken out of the boxes and the correct number of doves offered up.

Collecting box number five was for voluntary offerings for the wood used as the main fuel for the fires in the temple. Box number six was for money to buy incense for use in the temple. Incense itself could be presented, or it could be paid for as a voluntary offering. Collecting box seven was for contributions toward the temple's golden vessels, and boxes seven to thirteen were for various freewill offerings, such as Nazirite offerings and trespass offerings.

Anyone making a Nazirite vow was expected to make a freewill offering. A worshiper compelled to give a particular sum as a trespass offering usually gave more, and the excess was placed in one of these boxes. Most tithes were compulsory, but there were also voluntary second tithes, usually intended for help-

The Nazirite Chamber, set aside for those taking Nazirite vows.

ing the poor, which were placed in one of these collecting boxes. The money in these boxes was later presented at the temple.

As the boxes were trumpet shaped and made of metal, the rich made a noisy spectacle of their giving, so that onlookers noticed and thought how generous they were. The less well-off found it difficult to contribute to the temple, and probably came in quietly so as not to be noticed.

We can see that the Court of Prayer, added later by Herod, served many important functions, though it posed something of a bottleneck to the crowds passing through.

Opposite: **The main doors into the sanctuary.**

11. The Sanctuary: God's House

The temple sanctuary, pictured here as a separate building. In fact it was surrounded by many courts, as we have seen.

The temple sanctuary was the most important building on the temple site, since it was in the Most Holy Place within it that God dwelt, as he had done previously in the Holy of Holies in the tabernacle in the wilderness. The sanctuary stood on the west side of the Court of the Priests, of which area it occu-pied almost two-thirds. At its widest, the sanctuary was one hundred cubits, and at its highest, one hundred cubits. Approaching the temple sanctuary from the east, one first entered the porch built by Herod, which stood in front of the sanctuary itself. Behind this porch was the building, sixty cubits wide, that housed both the Holy Place and the Most Holy Place (or Holy of Holies).

On the south, west, and north sides of the sanctuary were thirty-eight chambers, in which the enormous wealth of the temple was stored. On the north side a staircase led up to the temple roof.

The temple was built of white limestone. Limestone, a low grade of marble, is found in and around Jerusalem. For ordinary building work, it would be quarried and rough-hewn; for fine work, it would be dressed and polished to a much finer finish. The temple sanctuary must have been built of white limestone and dressed to a fine finish, giving a gleaming white appearance; Josephus said that the temple gleamed white in the sunlight.

Gold spikes were fixed all around the top of the temple sanctuary roof. According to the Mishnah, their purpose was to deter birds from flying over and landing on the sanctuary and fouling it, thus making it ritually unclean. But it is hardly likely that gold railings, spikes, or ornaments would deter the birds. It is much more likely that men were posted on the roof of the temple sanctuary to prevent birds fouling it.

Of the various chambers within the temple, the Holy of Holies, at its west

end, was the most important. This chamber measured twenty cubits square by forty cubits high and, in Solomon's Temple, contained the ark of the covenant. When Solomon's Temple was destroyed, the ark was lost. This chamber was completely empty in Herod's Temple, apart from the rock on which the high priest sprinkled the blood on the Day of Atonement.

A veil or curtain divided the Holy Place from the Holy of Holies. This was suspended from the top and measured twenty cubits (about nine meters or thirty feet) wide and forty cubits (about eighteen meters or sixty feet) high. The veil was made up of seventy-two squares, woven on the temple site in the Chamber of the Curtain (where, as we have seen, eighty-two women were weaving continuously) and subsequently sewn together. Two completely new veils were made every year (*Shekalim* 8.5). This great veil was embroidered and woven in the temple colors: white, gold, blue, purple, and scarlet—the same as the tabernacle colors. In the Second Temple, it appears that there were two veils with a cubit's space between them (*Yoma* 5.1).

There were, in total, thirteen curtains in the temple. It is not clear exactly where all these were located; but in addition to the veil within the Holy Place and the Holy of Holies, a blue veil hung at the entrance of the Holy Place, another veil hung in the chamber above the Holy of Holies, and a veil hung at each of the ten entrances on the temple court.

There were three very important objects in the Holy Place: the altar of incense, the golden seven-branched lampstand, and the table of showbread. The altar of incense, on which the priest burned the incense, stood directly in front of the inner veil. The lampstand, which was kept burning continuously, was on the south side of the sanctuary; while the table of showbread stood on the north side of the sanctuary.

The Table of Showbread

The table of showbread (also known as the bread of the presence) was designed to display loaves of bread before God, as a sign of gratitude for his provision of food. The Old Testament (Exodus 25:23–30, 37:10–16) tells us it measured two cubits (0.9 meters or three feet) long by one cubit (0.45 meters or eighteen inches) wide and one cubit and a half (0.7 meters or two feet three inches) high and was made of wood overlaid with gold, with a gold rim around the outside, about a hand's-breadth (ten cm or four inches) wide. During the time of the tabernacle, the table also had rings attached for inserting carrying poles, so that it could be moved easily when necessary.

Two piles each of six loaves, supported by canes and golden staves, were placed on the table of showbread, as recorded in the Mishnah. The Mishnah also describes the table of showbread itself; the measurements vary slightly from those in Exodus, though the differences are not significant. The Mishnah explains how the loaves of bread were displayed and that they were changed every Sabbath, with the incoming priests bringing in fresh loaves and the outgoing priests taking away the old ones (*Menahoth* 11.5, 6).

The Seven-Branched Lampstand

This lampstand (Exodus 25:31–40, 37:17–24) stood on the south side of the Holy Place and was constructed with various bowls and with beaten metal ornamental work of knots, flowers, and branches. We have no measurements for the lampstand. The lamp burned continually, giving light in the Holy Place, tended by the priests on duty. The lampstand was made from one talent of solid gold, as were the lamps, snuffers, and snuff dishes. The relief in Rome on the triumphal Arch of Titus, the conqueror of Jerusalem, depicts the *menorah* (to give it its Hebrew name), as a distinctly different lampstand from that described in Exodus; either the original lampstand must have been replaced, or the sculptor exercised considerable artistic licence in his depiction.

The altar of incense

The altar of incense (Exodus 30:1–10, 37:25–28) stood just in front of the veil in the Holy Place of the temple, while the ark of the covenant stood behind the veil, inside the Holy of Holies. In the tabernacle, the altar of incense measured one cubit square and two cubits high, was made of wood overlaid with gold, and was fitted with poles to carry it when it had to be moved from place to place. (In the temple, the altar of incense remained stationary.) The sole function of this altar was, as its name suggests, to burn incense, whose sweet-smelling savor was thought to be essential in finding favor with God. It also created a holy atmosphere in which people could worship God. The priests burned incense on this altar as they carried out the morning and evening sacrifices and during sacrifices at the various annual festivals.

The Ark of the Covenant

The ark of the covenant (Exodus 25:10–22, 37:1–9) was the most sacred piece of temple furniture in the Jewish religion, but it *never* stood in the Holy of Holies in Herod's Temple. Moses was instructed how to make the ark and where to place it in the Holiest Place. The ark of the covenant was a wooden chest about two and a half cubits long by one and a half cubits square, overlaid with gold. Inside it were preserved the Ten Commandments inscribed on stone tablets, Aaron's rod, and a pot of manna. The lid of the chest, often referred to as the mercy seat, was surmounted with two cherubim, one on each end, facing each other, with their wings outstretched

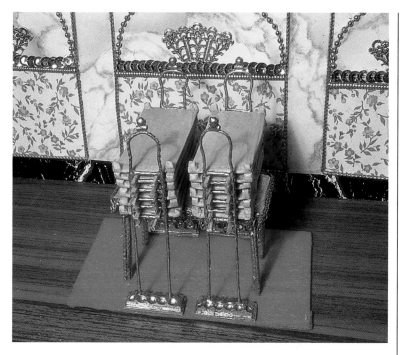

and touching. Carrying poles were attached to the sides of the ark, so that it could be moved when the children of Israel struck camp during their years of wandering in the wilderness. I have tried to reconstruct the ark's appearance as I understand it from these instructions.

The ark of the covenant had awesome power that enabled the children of Israel to win great victories and achieve remarkable feats throughout their his-

Top: The table of showbread, also known as the bread of the presence, designed to display loaves of bread before God.

Bottom: The lamps of the seven-branched lampstand burned continuously, giving light in the Holy Place. The lampstand was made from one talent (eighty-one pounds) of solid gold.

The altar of incense stood just in front of the veil in the Holy Place of the temple and was made of wood, overlaid with gold and designs. Its function was to burn incense, whose sweet-smelling savour was part of the ceremonial law essential for finding favor with God.

tory as a nation. The ark was placed in the Holy of Holies within the tabernacle, and when the children of Israel traveled through the wilderness, it was always carried ahead of them. When the Israelites finally crossed over the River Jordan from the wilderness into the Promised Land, the ark of the covenant went before them. As it was carried into the river, the waters parted, so the people were able to cross over on dry land.

As the Israelites advanced into Canaan, carrying the ark in front of them, they gradually took possession of what they believed to be their inheritance, given to them by God, defeating the inhabitants of the land. They captured the city of Jericho by carrying the ark around outside the walls each day for six days; then on the seventh day, after carrying it around seven times, they gave a great shout, and the walls collapsed (Joshua 6:15–20).

As the Israelites progressed through the Promised Land, the power contained in the ark did not always seem to go with them. They won many battles, but there were also occasions when they lost.

Sometimes the ark of the covenant was even captured by the Israelites' enemies, before eventually being recaptured. The Jewish people did not always march under God's favor, because at times they neglected, or disobeyed, the covenant that God had made with them.

Eventually, David, the great king of Israel, recaptured the ark and took it to Jerusalem, the new capital of his kingdom. Later Solomon built the First Temple and placed the ark of the covenant in the Holy of Holies (1 Kings 8). In the description of the ark at this time, we seem to have different specifications for the cherubim, as they now appear to stand apart from the ark. It is unclear whether the cherubim described are the cherubim that were formerly on the lid of the ark or additional cherubim.

Solomon's reign was prosperous but not long after came problems. The temple was looted by the Egyptians, who took away some of its treasures. After this time, we read nothing more in the Bible about the ark of the covenant, so we do not know if it still existed. Finally the Babylonians conquered and overran Israel, destroying the temple, and taking away all its treasures (2 Kings 25).

We do not know if a fate similar to that of the ark of the covenant befell the seven-branched lampstand, the table of showbread, and the altar of incense. But we do know that reconstructions of these sacred furnishings stood in Herod's Temple. It is most unlikely that there was a reproduction of the ark of the covenant in Herod's Temple.

The Porch

As we have seen above, a magnificent porch stood in front of the east entrance of the temple sanctuary in Herod's time. Before this entrance stood four columns ornamented with a golden vine. The Mishnah gives an elaborate description of the size, weight, and value of the vine and its fruit (*Middot* 3.8). A worshiper could buy a golden grape or leaf in the

Two priests maintain the Holy Place. The man on the left is trimming the lamps of the seven-branched lampstand; the man on the right is looking after the altar of incense, which stands immediately in front of the great veil, or curtain, dividing off the Holy of Holies.

market outside, where priests sold all sorts of commodities for temple offerings and sacrifices, and have it suspended on the vine. Golden chains hung down from the top of the porch, and a young priest would climb up one of these chains and hang up the grapes or the leaves that the worshipers had presented to the temple.

North and south of this main entrance to the sanctuary were two Chambers of the Utensils, where the knives, bowls, and other equipment required for carrying out the sacrifices were stored.

Two tables, one of marble, the other of gold, stood in this porch in front of the sanctuary. Before the showbread was taken into the Holy Place, it was placed on the marble table; when it was brought out of the sanctuary a week later, it was

Top and bottom: **Eighty-two young women were kept busy weaving, sewing, and washing the seventy-two pieces which made up the two veils dividing the Holy Place from the Holy of Holies.**

placed on the gold table. It was then removed and the new showbread was taken into the sanctuary. The priests serving in the temple that particular week ate the discarded showbread.

Twelve steps descended in sets of three from the sanctuary entrance, each set followed by a wide platform known as a terrace. (The Mishnah refers to the terraces, or landings, on this flight of steps.) The temple porch had no door, but five huge carved and decorated beams surmounted it, with courses of stones between them.

12. The Antonia Fortress

The Antonia Fortress replaced the earlier Hasmonean Baris Tower when Herod extended and rebuilt the temple. The Baris Tower stood at the northwest corner of the five-hundred-cubit-square Temple Mount and was connected to it by an underground passage (Chamber 1 in Warren's numbering). There has always been some confusion about this tunnel, because some people claim that it continued as far as the Antonia Fortress. There appears to be no evidence to support this.

Just east of the Antonia Fortress, in an open area, was the Pool of Israel, where sheep for sacrifice were brought to be washed. After being washed and prepared for slaughter, the sheep were taken into the temple. Between the Pool of Israel and the Antonia Fortress was the northern gate of the temple, where people habitually gathered.

A stairway led down from the Antonia Fortress into the northwest courtyard of the temple, which was part of Herod's addition to the temple site. Josephus states that there were grand, even palatial, buildings within the Antonia Fortress, with bathing and washing facilities (*War* 4:5–8). It is possible that the Roman governor, Pontius Pilate, stayed here when he visited Jerusalem.

The Antonia Fortress stood just outside the north boundary of the temple site, near the northern porch. It stood on a raised rock-hewn platform, about twenty cubits above the temple platform, which can still be seen today beneath modern buildings. This platform is about two hundred and seventy cubits long by eighty cubits wide. Using Josephus's description, we can judge how the rock was squared off to form this platform on which the fortress was built.

The Pool of Israel, where sheep for sacrifice were brought to be washed. In the background stands the Antonia Fortress.

Bird's-eye view of Herod's Temple from the east, showing clearly the arrangement of the courts.

Top: **The Antonia Fortress, named for Herod the Great's patron, Mark Antony.**

Bottom: **Bird's-eye view of the inner court of the Antonia Fortress.**

Josephus records,

"the Antonia Tower lay at the north-western corner of the temple's outer court. Built by King Herod, it rose forty cubits from a rock base fifty cubits in height, and its interior resembled a palace in its spaciousness and furnishings, with accommodation and broad courtyards also for troops. Towers rose at each of its four corners, the one at the southeast reaching seventy cubits in height and commanding a view of the entire temple area. Stairs led down to the temple porticoes where they impinged on the Antonia, by which the guards descended. A Roman cohort was quartered there permanently, and posted around the porticoes at the festivals to watch the people and repress any rebellions. For if the temple controlled the city, the Antonia dominated the temple . . ." (*War* 5:238–246).

The Antonia was in fact a rebuilding of the earlier Baris Fortress, which had stood on the northwest corner of the earlier square Temple Mount, on the same site as the Mea and Hananeel towers mentioned in the book of Nehemiah. Herod named the fortress after Mark Antony, the Roman ruler who had originally promoted him to power. This dedication must date from before the Battle of Actium, 31 B.C., since Herod would not have honored him in this way after Antony's defeat by Octavian.

Various theories have been put forward regarding the location of the Antonia Fortress described by Josephus. Père Benoît proposed the approximately four hundred-foot rock scarp on which the Ommariya school now stands, and this has now been generally approved. Michael Burgoyne, in his recent research on Mamluk Jerusalem, even identified a remnant of the south wall of the Antonia in the south walls of the Ommariya school. A large buttress from the fortress has also been discovered during tunnel excavations carried out near the Western Wall by the Ministry of Religious Affairs.

The staircase mentioned by Josephus that led up from the Temple Mount to the Antonia Fortress formed the backdrop to the scene when Paul defended himself in Hebrew against his countrymen (Acts 21–22); and it was in the courtyard of this fortress that Paul was bound with cords and prepared for scourging.

13. The Chambers Beneath the Temple

There is an unknown number of chambers, tunnels, and similar structures beneath the temple platform. The Victorian surveyor Sir Charles Warren located thirty-seven, all of which are indicated on the diagram on page 81. Most of these chambers were to provide access to particular parts of the temple or for the storage of water.

Some of these chambers are especially significant to our study of the temple, while some are of less interest and may date from long before Herod's time. We consider below the more relevant of these underground chambers.

Chamber 1 was a passage leading from the Court of the Priests north across the five-hundred-cubit square, with its exit just on the edge of the square. This passage led into and out of the temple, and was possibly used for discreet access.

Chamber 2 was also located in the five-hundred-cubit square northeast of the Temple Mount, within the Court of Israel. Its function is unknown, but it was possibly used for ritual washing.

Chamber 3 was certainly used for ritual washing and for toilets. It connects on the west with one side of Passage 1 and was entered via a descending staircase from the Chamber of the Hearth, where the priests lived while on duty. A fire was kept burning here, and the priests could wash and warm themselves before returning to duty.

Chamber 4, on the west side of the temple, was small, and its purpose is unknown.

Chamber 5 is very significant for our reconstruction of the temple. Hewn from the rock, it formed an underground passage beneath the edge of the temple court, directly below the wheel that drew up water for the laver.

Chamber 6 was smaller and lay to the south, though still within the original five-hundred-cubit square Temple Mount. This chamber may have served as a sacred washing place for the public visiting the temple. Chamber 36, close by and slightly larger, was almost the same shape and was used for similar purposes. Perhaps the smaller Chamber 6 provided washing facilities and toilets for women, while Chamber 36 provided similar facilities for men.

Chamber 7 was a large water storage chamber under the temple site, located in the Herodian extensions, and fed with surface water as well as by a viaduct from Solomon's Pools, near Bethlehem.

Chamber 8 was a similar, very large cistern, perhaps the largest on the temple site. It was sometimes called the Great Sea and provided water for general use in the temple.

Chamber 9, quite close to Chamber 8, was another large chamber that stored water for the day-to-day requirements of various parts of the temple. Chambers 7, 8, and 9 were all situated under the Herodian extensions in the south part of the temple, between the five-hundred-cubit square and the Royal Porch.

Chamber 10 was under the Royal Porch and almost directly beneath the Triple Gate. It was a rock-hewn tunnel leading off at an angle, but its function is unclear.

Chamber 11 was further into the tem-

Two priests immerse themselves for ritual cleansing in the baths inside the Chamber of the Hearth.

ple, under the passage that led from the Triple Gate, and was also a cistern providing water for the buildings above.

Chambers 12, 13, and *14* were situated at the east end of the Temple Mount. Chambers 13 and 14 were on the Temple Mount, and chamber 12 was within the Temple Court, just under the Chamber of the Wood. All three were medium sized and may have been used for storage or washing.

Chamber 15 was small and just inside the Eastern Gate (now known as the Golden Gate) within the Temple Mount. Its function is unknown.

Chambers 16 and 17 were on the north edge of the temple site, just inside the wall by the Pool of Israel, and probably date from before the time of Herod the Great.

Chamber 18, in the northwest corner, was connected by a cut channel to the Strouthion Pool just outside the Temple Mount and supplied water to the Antonia Fortress.

Chamber 19 was at the south end of the Western Wall, where much excavation has taken place in recent years. This was the entrance for a low-level gate that led into the temple site, known today as Barclay's Gate.

Chamber 20 was closely connected to Chamber 19 and must have served that

entrance in some way.

Chamber 21 was situated just inside the north edge of the temple site, quite near the Pool of Israel, and close to Chambers 16 and 17. Its purpose is unclear.

Chamber 22 was quite large, and again near Chamber 18, toward the north end of the Western Wall. It was used to store water for that part of the temple site and probably predates the temple extensions there.

Chamber 23 was just outside the northeast corner of the Temple Mount and probably served a previous building such as a tower.

Chamber 24 was a relatively modern chamber, just inside the Temple Mount.

Chamber 25 was situated close to Chamber 24, on the west side of the Temple Mount; it was small and of little importance.

Chamber 26, on the north edge of the temple site, in the Herodian extensions near the Pool of Israel but inside the temple site, was closely connected to Chambers 16, 17, and 21.

Chamber 27, also on the northern edge just inside the Antonia Fortress, was a small chamber, probably for storing water.

Chamber 28 was a small chamber on the northeast corner of the five-hundred-cubit square.

Chamber 29, just outside the north edge of the five-hundred-cubit square, consisted of a series of small chambers and probably dated from the Crusader period.

Chamber 30 was very important, being the passage that led from Warren's Gate the low-level entrance similar to and north of Barclay's Gate, into the temple from the west side. Today it leads in from the tunnel excavated by Dan Bahat, which goes partway into the temple site. Nobody knows exactly where it goes, and the Muslims have sealed it off; but it probably leads right under the sacred area of the temple, through the boundary wall of Solomon's Temple.

Chamber 31 was a small cistern, cen-

Underground Chambers of the Temple

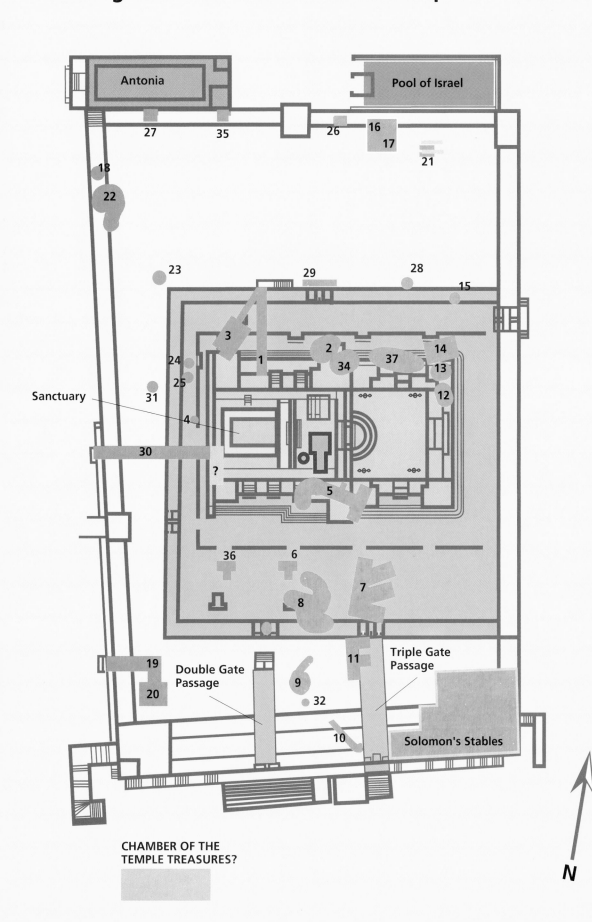

Antonia

Pool of Israel

27   35   26   16
            17
            21

18
22

23   29   28   15

3
24   1   2   34   37   14
25   13
31   12

Sanctuary
4
30
?   5

36   6

7
8

19   Double Gate
Passage   11   Triple Gate
Passage

20   9   32

10   Solomon's Stables

CHAMBER OF THE
TEMPLE TREASURES?

N

Tunnels beneath the
Temple Mount.

trally situated just inside the Western
Wall, but just outside the five-hundred-
cubit square.

Chamber 32 was a small chamber in
the southern part of the temple site, just
on the edge of the Royal Porch, and near
the passageway that led to the Double
Gate.

Chamber 33 was quite near and under-
neath the passage of the Royal Porch,
which led to the Double Gate. It is pre-
sumably now under the floor of al-Aqsa.

Chamber 34 was one of a little group
of chambers—2, 34, and 37—outside the
temple court on the north wall, close to
the Court of the Women.

Chamber 35, by the extreme north wall
of the temple site, and adjoining the
Antonia Fortress, was small and
insignificant.

Chambers 36 and *6* (see above) were
close together. Chamber 36 was within
the five-hundred-cubit square and the
larger of these two sacred baths.

Chamber 37 was close to Chambers 34
and 2, directly under the Chamber of the
Wood.

This completes our survey of the chambers on the Temple Mount numbered by
Warren, but we should consider some
other features. Located at the far southeast corner of the temple are the so-called
Solomon's Stables, underground chambers that actually had nothing to do with
King Solomon. These were vaults built
on the temple site, destroyed by the
Romans in A.D. 70, and later rebuilt by
the Crusaders, who stabled their horses
there. Farther along the south side was
a passage, part of which still remains,
that led to the modern Triple Gate.

A little further west along the south
side of the Temple Mount was a passage
that led from the Double Gate, now
partly covered over by a building from
the Crusader period. The entrances
themselves remain, together with part
of the (unnumbered) passage and its ceiling.

Some of the chambers described
above are important in providing information about the construction of the
temple. For instance, Chamber 1 links
up with the original buildings; Chamber
3 was the washing place; Chamber 5
links with the drawing of water for the
laver; Chambers 7, 8, and 9 were for
water storage; Chambers 6 and 36 were
washing places which were located
exactly where we would expect to find
them; Chamber 19 leads to the low-level
Barclay's Gate; and Chamber 30 leads
from Warren's Gate.

14. Feasts and Festivals in the Temple

What happened on a normal day in the temple? At cockcrow (about 3:00 A.M.) the priests began to prepare for the morning sacrifice of a lamb. At the Place of Trumpeting, the priest on duty gave the signal for the lamb to be sacrificed when the outline of the Hebron mountains became visible. The Eastern, or Nicanor, Gate was then opened for the worshipers to meet the priests, and another day began in the temple.

People on pilgrimage from abroad, who wished to worship in the temple, brought gifts, offerings, and sacrifices.

People met their friends and ate a sacramental meal together, celebrating, worshiping, and glorifying God. Women came to be cleansed from childbirth, others came to take the Nazirite vow, and many activities went on. It was always busy.

There were many special feast days at the temple, too. Originally every Jew was obliged to attend three main festivals, according to the Law of Moses. By the time of Herod's Temple, many more feast days had been added. According to the ancient document *Megillath Taanith* (the Scroll of Fasting), some thirty-five spe-

The Temple illuminated by night. It would have appeared like this during the Feast of Tabernacles, following the water-drawing ceremony.

cial feast and fast days took place on Temple Mount. Of course, the Jewish authorities in charge were aware that the more special days there were, the more money would be brought into the temple. There were festivals such as New Moon, the Blowing of Trumpets, and the Sabbath, besides all the feasting, fasting, and celebrating that normally went on in the temple.

Passover

Passover was perhaps the most important festival. These special celebrations usually lasted several days, sometimes as long as seven or eight days. Passover marked the start of the festive season, and lasted only half a day; from midday until midnight from 14 to 15 of the Jewish month of Nisan. People would select a lamb and have it inspected and prepared, to make sure it qualified as a Passover lamb. Then they would bring it to be sacrificed in the temple, before taking it to eat in their own homes.

At about 3.00 P.M., people brought their lambs to the Nicanor Gate, where they were sacrificed. At least five hundred priests were on duty, because so many lambs were presented and there was limited time available to carry out the sacrifices. The lambs had to be slaughtered within the temple in the required manner. Each was killed by cutting its throat, and its blood was caught and sprinkled at the base of the altar. This was done as quickly as possible, so the next could come to take its place. One group came into the Court of Prayer, and when it was full of worshipers, the doors were closed and that group was attended to (*Pesahim* 5.5). Then another group was allowed in. Considering the size of this area and the time available, the number of lambs slaughtered could not have been more than about thirty thousand, though that was still a huge number.

Anyone who has seen a lamb slaughtered in this way will know that bleeding does not stop immediately, and the creature does not die straightaway. Blood would be flowing all over the Court of the Priests and the Court of the Women. When it was all over, the priests swilled down the courts to wash away all the blood. It must have been a stomach wrenching sight.

First Day of Unleavened Bread

Many people confuse the First Day of Unleavened Bread with Passover itself, which it followed. On this day, there were special sacrifices, celebration, and rejoicing. The people recalled how God had redeemed his people through the Passover lamb, originally sacrificed in Egypt, and supplied all their needs as they traveled through the wilderness. This festival marked the barley harvest with special sacrifices, and there were seven days of unleavened bread, all special days of sacrifice and celebration.

Passover itself was regarded as a Sabbath, and the First Day of Unleavened Bread as a special feast day and a time of sacrifice. The remaining days of the week were important but not held in such high regard as Passover and the First Day. The Feast of Unleavened Bread did not really finish until Pentecost, seven weeks later.

Day of Pentecost

The Day of Pentecost was also a very special celebration, and it concluded the Feast of Unleavened Bread. In this feast the people offered up two loaves and two lambs. The loaves were made of leavened flour, to form a wave offering which was offered to God by being waved in front of the altar, then received back. This festival celebrated the wheat harvest.

People brought thank-offerings, and special sacrifices and services were prescribed for the day. After the wave offering, the people brought their gifts and offerings to the priests in the temple. On the Day of Pentecost, proselytes—for eign people who wanted to take up the ewish religion—were baptized, following a tradition that had developed over he years.

Tabernacles

The third obligatory festival was Tabernacles. This too was a succession of feast days, beginning on the first day of the seventh month, which was also he first day of the New Year. On New Year's Day, the people celebrated New Moons and Trumpets, followed later by he Day of Atonement. During this feast, which followed the ceremony of water-drawing, the great lampstands were lit n the temple.

Day of Atonement

On the Day of Atonement, a time of great solemnity when the people sought God's forgiveness and acceptance, there was a special sacrifice. The high priest carried ut special services and ordinances, and wo goats and two bulls were sacrificed n particular ways. The bulls were laughtered—one to atone for the priests, he other to atone for the people—and heir blood was sprinkled on the altar nd the furnishings in the temple.

One of the goats was slaughtered, its blood mixed with the blood of one of the bulls, and then sprinkled in the temple. The other goat, the scapegoat symbolically carrying the sins of the people, was aken out onto the Mount of Olives in a very elaborate procedure, through the emple gate that led into the Kidron Valley, to wander off into the wilderness nd die.

On this day, too, the high priest went nto the Holy of Holies and sprinkled blood before the veil and on the rock here. As we have noted previously, he ad to wash in a sacred bath, change his arments five times, and wash his hands nd feet ten times. This solemn and elaborate ceremony went on all day. When it vas completed, and atonement was

During the Feast of Tabernacles the golden lampstands were lit.

achieved at the end of the day, great rejoicing and celebration ensued in the temple.

Feast of Tabernacles

Five days later came the Feast of Tabernacles, sometimes called the Great Feast, when special offerings and sacrifices were made. Each day, for the six days of the Feast of Tabernacles, the high priest took into the temple a golden ewer of water drawn from the Pool of Siloam and sprinkled the water around the altar. On the seventh day, he walked seven times around the altar, splashing it with water all the while.

A red heifer is led out of the Eastern Gate toward the Mount of Olives.

Bulls too were slaughtered for this feast, a different number on each day; and on the final and greatest day, the lights in the temple were lit, and great celebrations followed. Tabernacles was a time when the people could rejoice and give thanks for God's provision of all fruit and grain, and everything else they needed. It was a time of great praise and rejoicing, which on the last day continued through the night until cockcrow, at 3.00 A.M.

The Mishnah describes it vividly. "At the close of the first Festival Day of the Feast they went down to the Court of the Women where they had made a great change. There were golden candlesticks there with four golden bowls on top of them and four ladders to each candlestick, and four youths of the priestly stock and in their hands jars of oil holding a hundred and twenty logs* which they poured into the bowls. They made wicks from the worn out drawers and girdles of the priests and with them they set the candlesticks alight, and there was not a courtyard in Jerusalem that did not reflect the light . . . Men of piety and good works danced before them with burning torches in their hands, singing songs and praises" (*Sukkah* 5.1–4).

It has been suggested that when Jesu said, during the Feast of Tabernacles, ' am the light of the world" (John 8:12), h was alluding to these impressive illum nations.

These festivals were all fixed accord ing to the lunar calendar, so they did no take place on exactly the same day eac year. They varied according to the tim of the new moon, just as the Christia Easter occurs on a different date in th calendar each year.

Sacrifice of the Red Heifer

Besides these three or four major annu festivals, another ceremony took plac more rarely. This was the sacrifice of th red heifer to provide the ashes used fc purification, particularly for the priest This was only done when the supply ashes ran low and, in fact, took place onl twelve times in the whole history of Israel. The red heifer was led out of th gate on the east side of the temple, acro the Kidron Valley, and on to the Mou of Olives, where it was slaughtered.

At that moment, the high priest looke back toward the temple. He could se

* A log was a liquid measurement, approximately equivalent to 0.3 liters.

Women were lit only three times a year. One occasion was before the Feast of the Dedication of the Temple, which marked the liberation of the temple from the Greeks in the time of Judas Maccabeus. They celebrated the Festival of Lights for eight days beginning on the twenty-fifth day in the ninth month of the Jewish calendar (Kislev, our December).

These celebrations and festivals, of which there are many, brought in much wealth to the temple. The provision of sacrificial animals formed the basis of an enormous trade that helped support the economy of the whole country.

Sabbath

In addition to these special festivals, each month brought a new moon and each week a Sabbath. Because of the Sabbath laws and restrictions, there were fewer worshipers at these times, which enabled the priests to carry out such special duties as cleaning the altar and changing over the showbread.

The priests changed over duties on the Sabbath. The incoming priests brought in the new showbread loaves and placed them on the marble table in the porch, just outside the Holy Place. Then the priests who were leaving took out the old loaves and put them on the golden table on the south side of the porch, and the new loaves were taken in. The outgoing priests were allowed to eat the showbread that had been placed in the temple that week, a great privilege. They conducted the morning sacrifice before they left, leaving the incoming priests to conduct the evening sacrifice.

This is just a brief summary of the way that the temple operated. While the priests carried out the privileged duties, the Levites, as the temple guard, kept law and order and made sure that all the temple rules were observed.

over its eastern wall and through the Eastern Gate into the temple itself. As he gazed in the direction of the temple, he sprinkled the animal's blood toward the temple. The red heifer was then surrounded with wood and faggots, set on fire, and burned to ashes, which were mixed with water, gathered together, and put into containers. One container was placed on the Mount of Olives, one on the terrace by the Gate of the Pure and the Just, and one inside the temple sanctuary. These ashes were sprinkled on the priests as a remedy for ritual uncleanness and defilement, especially when they came on duty, and if they had been defiled by contact with a corpse.

Dedication of the Temple

According to the Mishnah, the four giant lamps that stood in the Court of the

15. Who Ran the Temple?

When we recognize just how large Herod's Temple was, we see how much organization must have been necessary to run it. Everything had to work smoothly and efficiently.

The Priests

The priests were the most important people in the temple and comprised various ranks, orders, and tribes, with different priests on duty at different times.

To perform his duties, a priest had to reach a certain standard of education and also had to be married, as he did to qualify for membership of the Sanhedrin Council. Not all those qualified by birth for the priesthood were accepted; those afflicted by physical disability or some other form of "uncleanness" were prevented from serving. Although membership of the priesthood was hereditary, corruption crept in; in Herod's day, it was in fact possible to buy one's way into the priesthood. The temptation to do this was great; once appointed a priest, a man could use his authority to make large sums of money.

The high priest was the most important man in Israel, occupying every leading official position, presiding over every major operation, and making every final decision. Even the king was normally subject to the high priest's rule. In Herod's time, however, this hierarchy changed, as the high priest came under Rome's authority. Herod the Great had relatively more authority than most kings of Israel. Other officials held important positions under the high priest and were responsible for subsidiary matters.

The Sadducees

Most of the higher ranks within the priesthood were occupied by Sadducees. Despite being a religious building, the temple was the center of *all* Jewish life; all major decisions, including those concerning the control and organization of the entire land, were made there. The temple and its institutions formed a major portion of the country's economy and brought in vast sums of money. This provided the leaders, such as the high priest and the Sadducees, with very comfortable positions. The Sadducees did not object to being under Rome's authority, as they were naturally in favor of the *status quo* and were very wealthy. The Sadducees looked forward to a time when Israel would be a great world power.

The Levites

The Levites, like the priests, held highly favored hereditary positions, though at a lower level. They formed part of the temple guard, responsible for strictly enforcing the temple laws and regulations. Some guards were priests, as certain parts of the temple could not be entered by Levites to enforce the law. Anyone who violated these temple laws was severely dealt with; the temple guards showed little mercy.

The Levites also were responsible for music and singing in the temple, a key part of the worship there. They played

The high priest in the Holy Place, holding the Torah. Behind him is the golden lampstand.

various musical instruments and sang, leading worship from the semicircular platform at the top of the fifteen Steps of Ascent. The Levite musicians trained for their roles from early ages, and their skills at harmonizing the voices of older and younger men with the musical instruments were renowned throughout the ancient world.

The Levites were excluded from authority over the sacrificial market in the outer courts of the temple, which was under the control of Annas the high priest during Herod's time. (The sacrificial market should not be confused with the general commercial market outside the temple.) Annas was in effect high priest *emeritus*, and he tightly controlled the market and much of the priesthood at this time, and was consequently extremely wealthy.

The Pharisees

The Pharisees could easily be distinguished in the temple by their modest-looking dress, which was less elaborate than the Sadducees' fine clothing. The Pharisees gained their positions by study, devotion, and learning. They strove to obey every detail of the Law as they understood it. They were largely responsible for writing the Mishnah.

The Pharisees stressed the Law of God and fulfilling the covenant in a very practical way, keeping the letter of the Law in every tiny detail. They stopped at the street corner or in the market to fulfil what they believed to be the Law's requirements for prayer and benediction but tended to disregard the spirit of the Law. They wore special garments and phylacteries (leather boxes containing Scripture verses) and cut their hair in a special way. While some people revered the Pharisees, others feared and hated them.

The Essenes

The Essenes, a less known group, were more concerned with keeping the spirit of the Law and rarely entered the temple—or even Jerusalem. They had their own community at Qumran, near the Dead Sea, where they practised their own style of worship. They did not sacrifice animals but kept the covenant of God in their own way by prayers and devotional worship.

A rabbi helps a Jewish boy read from the Torah at the Western Wall, Jerusalem.

Opposite: **A scene at the Western Wall, a holy place for the Jews, since it is the only accessible remnant of the Temple Mount dating from biblical times. The lower masonry dates from the Herodian period.**

Scribes

There were two types of scribe. Temple scribes worked in the Chamber of the Stone (the Chamber of the Honorable Councillors), copying the Scriptures continually and fulfiling other duties connected with the temple worship.

Other scribes provided a public letter-writing service. Such a scribe carried a quill pen and other writing equipment with him, ready to read or write letters for anyone who would pay the fee.

Elders

Elders were, as the name suggests, older citizens—sages and wise men—with all their accumulated wisdom, learning, and sayings.

The Lawyers

The lawyers in the temple were very different from modern lawyers. Although they had a sophisticated legal system, there were no appeals. If someone was accused of wrongdoing, he was dealt with quickly and severely.

These lawyers were able to interpret the Law of Moses, which many ordinary people did not fully understand. If someone had a problem, he asked one of these learned men, who might also be an elder, a scribe, or a Pharisee.

The Rabbis

Another prominent group in the temple was the rabbis. A rabbi could be a scribe or Pharisee and was a traveling teacher. Some rabbis were brought up in the Jewish schools, after which they sat at the feet of well-known scholars in the temple, as the apostle Paul did (Acts 22:3). Paul fully understood the Jewish law and could preach and teach. Other rabbis were just ordinary people who had something they wanted to proclaim; they taught people in the street, in the temple, or at some other place reserved for them. A rabbi had to be of some competence before he could teach in Solomon's Porch or in the treasury. He had to sit among the senior rabbis. Many of them improved their qualifications, and thus their authority, as they gained a larger following.

These then are the main groups of people who organized and ran the temple. The priests monopolized the major jobs; for instance, priests were in charge of the gates, the treasury, and the running of the services.

Meanwhile, ordinary people—worshipers, street traders and shopkeepers—brought their goods to a site outside the temple to sell to the crowds of worshipers who continually arrived. All this amounted to a considerable trade, which was needed to run the temple. Porters offered their services to carry whatever needed moving.

16. Where Is the Lost Ark?

The Mishnah tells us that the ark of the covenant was hidden under the Wood Chamber (*Shekalim* 6.1–2). But the chambers surrounding this have been explored, and nothing has been found.

My research, however, has revealed new facts. In Herod's time, the Wood Chamber was at the northeast corner of the Court of Prayer, and wood for the fires in the temple was brought and stored here. But the Wood Gate was at the southwest corner of the Court of the Priests, diagonally across the Temple Court and at its far corner. I have long been puzzled as to why the Wood Gate and the Wood Chamber were situated so far apart. How did the priests transfer wood from the Wood Gate to the Wood Chamber? The answer is that they did not! In Herod's time, the wood was taken straight to the Wood Chamber, at the northeast corner of the Court of Prayer.

When Solomon's Temple was destroyed, the Wood Chamber was not where we understand it to have been in Herod's Temple, but close to the Wood Gate. People brought their offerings of wood to the Wood Gate, where it would have been stored on the ground floor. So when the ark of the covenant was hidden, the Wood Chamber was located in the southwest corner of the Court of the Priests. I believe the Mishnah's reference speaks of the original Wood Chamber, in the southwest corner, not the later, Herodian, Wood Chamber, in the northeast corner of the Temple Mount.

Because the Dome of the Rock stands on this site today, and the Muslims exercise control over it, it is very difficult to explore this area.

Since the Wood Chamber was on the south side of the temple in Solomon's time, it is not far from Warren's Gate, where extensive exploration has been carried out. However, because of Muslim sensitivity, work has now come to a stop, and we still do not know for certain what may be hidden there. Warren's Gate formed part of the Herodian extensions and was not part of Solomon's Temple. The tunnel under here has been partially excavated, and some scholars have concluded that it runs straight ahead (the present author's opinion), while others think it turns south at a right angle into the outer courts.

I believe there was a gate here in the wall of Solomon's Temple leading to a passage that went into the temple and the chambers under the Stone Chamber (which in Solomon's time was the Wood Chamber). It would have been in the lower part of the building, because the high priest lived in the upper part when he lodged in the temple. Dan Bahat, who has excavated extensively in this area, agrees with me that there must be chambers in this position under the temple site. Nobody has been able to explore them—although some claim to have done so, without being able to prove it.

In his book *Return to Sodom and Gomorrah* (1994), Charles Pellegrino refers to a claim made by three rabbis that they tunneled under Warren's Gate in 1981 and found chambers there. They claim that Solomon's treasures were hid-

den there and took a few fuzzy photographs, which admittedly look like treasures that might have belonged to Solomon's Temple. Rabbis Shlomo Goren and Yehuda Getz claim that, while digging there, they saw some objects that looked like the temple treasures but were stopped by Arab guards, who started a riot. The tunnel was then sealed off, and they were not allowed to enter. Shortly after this, in 1981, the Israeli government sealed off the whole area to prevent unrest.

Many people who have visited me and expressed interest in the temple model claim that they have seen, or been informed about, this area of the temple where the treasure is said to be hidden. I have not taken them seriously as they have no evidence. However, considering the position of the Wood Chamber, what the Mishnah says, and what other explorers have discovered, I am convinced that this must have been where the ark of the covenant was hidden.

When Jerusalem was attacked, it would have been difficult for the invaders to force an entry into the temple, so the delay would have allowed time for the priests to hide the ark of the covenant. Chambers were probably prepared in advance for just such an event. The ark of the covenant was probably hidden and then sealed up to prevent anyone finding it. In his book *Ready to Rebuild*, Randall Price makes claims similar to those of Charles Pellegrino.

We do not know if the ark is still concealed there today, though I believe that many of the temple treasures were originally hidden in this place. However, if the Mishnah says clearly that the ark was concealed here, why was it not subsequently recovered and put on display? Perhaps there is a good reason for this, or perhaps the ark was never hidden here in the first place. It might also have been hidden there originally, then moved or stolen—nobody knows where to.

The location of the ark of the covenant was remembered by tradition, which became distorted after a long lapse of time, though there would always have been some truth in the record. Only

The ark is not mentioned in the Scriptures after Solomon's reign.

much later would the tradition have been committed to writing. The Mishnah in general use today, written during the period 200 B.C. to A.D. 400, is a collection of writings, sayings, traditions, rules, and regulations collected by the rabbis. The Mishnah does not distinguish dates and times and refers to one temple in one verse and to a later temple in the next, without distinguishing between them. For example, the Mishnah sometimes refers to the tabernacle as if it still existed, so we have to be very careful when we read it. When the Mishnah refers to the Wood Chamber as the hiding place for the ark, it means the Wood Chamber that existed in Solomon's time.

Like other buildings in ancient times, the temple would have had secret chambers beneath it in which to store treasures or anything else that needed concealing. We know, for instance, that there were chambers under Egyptian tombs and under the pyramids where many treasures have been discovered. The same was true of many Greek and Roman buildings, so it is likely to have been true of Solomon's Temple too.

I don't know how the knowledge of the ark's location was lost. It may have been forgotten over a long period of time, or people may not have known how to reach it because there was so much rubble after the destruction of the temple. Perhaps it was felt that, for religious or other reasons, it was best to leave it undisturbed. Whatever the truth is, the fact remains that the ark is not mentioned in the Bible after Solomon's reign.

When Solomon's son Rehoboam came to the throne and the temple was plundered by the Egyptians, many of the valuable temple treasures were taken away and replaced with brass replicas. Those who knew of the ark's whereabouts possibly did not wish to reveal it. As with other hidden or lost treasures in Egypt or Greece, people occasionally would have discovered some treasure or perhaps plundered at some time for their money or religious value.

Ultimately, we do not know what, if anything, is hidden under this part of the temple, but it was almost certainly the original hiding place of the ark of the covenant. Some people think it may still be there, but nobody really knows what happened to it.

Index

Page numbers in italics denote illustrations.

Select Bibliography

Bahat, Dan. *The Illustrated Atlas of Jerusalem.* Lambda, 1990.

de Vaux, Roland. *Ancient Israel: Its Life and Institutions*, Grand Rapids, Mich.: Wm. B. Eerdmans, 1995.

Edersheim, Alfred. *The Temple: Its Ministry and Services as they were at the Time of Jesus*, ed. John J. Bimson. Grand Rapids, Mich.: Kregel Publications, 1997.

Gibson, Shimon and Jacobson, David M. *Below the Temple Mount in Jerusalem*, Washington, DC: Biblical Archaeology Society, 1996.

Ice, Thomas, Price, J. Randall, Ice, Tommy. *Ready to Rebuild: The Imminent Plan to Rebuild the Last Days Temple*, Eugene, Ore: Harvest House, 1992.

Josephus. *The New Complete Works of Josephus.* William Whiston, trans. Paul L. Maier, commentary. Kregel Publications, 1998.

Maier, Paul L. *Josephus: The Essential Works.* Grand Rapids, Mich.: Kregel Publications, 1994.

Mishnah, The, translated by Herbert Danby. Oxford: Clarendon Press, 1933.

Patrich, Joseph: 'The Mesibbah of the Temple According to the Tractate Middot', *Eretz*, spring 1987, Givatayim, Israel.

Pellegrino, Charles. *Return to Sodom and Gomorrah.* Avon Books, 1995

Price, J. Randall. *The Coming Last Days Temple*, Eugene Ore.: Harvest House, 1999.

Ritmeyer, Kathleen and L.P. *Secrets of Jerusalem's Temple Mount.* Washington, DC: Biblical Archaeology Society, 1998

Ritmeyer, L.P. *"The Architectural Development of the Temple Mount in Jerusalem".* Ph.D. diss., University of Manchester, England, 1992.

Yadin, Yigael. *The Temple Scroll: The Hidden Law of the Dead Sea Sect.* London: Weidenfeld & Nicolson, 1985